CONTENTS

INTRODUCTION

TOM SLATER

2020 will go down in history for all the wrong reasons.

The year began on a note of hope. After nearly four years of elite attempts to overturn the vote for Brexit, Britain finally, formally, left the EU. The establishment's refusal to honour the largest democratic mandate in British history had both poisoned and paralysed our politics. Finally we could look to the future again.

But as thousands gathered in Parliament Square on 31 January to cheer Brexit and what it represented – a blow for democracy against the ruling class, the re-energisation of public life after decades of ordinary people being shut out – fate was conspiring to put us all back in our box.

By the end of March, the UK was following much of the world into lockdown, as governments panicked in the face of a novel and deadly virus. While debate will rage for years about the efficacy of lockdown in fighting Covid-19, the toll it has taken on our society has been profound.

Civil liberties were suspended, parliaments packed up and went home, social life was replaced by social distancing, and we were plunged into the deepest recession in the history of modern capitalism, as the world embarked on an unprecedented experiment in authoritarianism.

Wishful thinking that this new external threat might at least cultivate a sense of shared purpose, a sense of solidarity often lacking in recent years, was soon shattered by another world-historical event: the murder of George Floyd by police in Minneapolis and the global discord that followed.

Woke identity politics exploded. Public anger at the killing of an unarmed black man was eclipsed by elite hysteria about the 'original sin' of racism. Concerns about racial inequality were edged out by a campaign of cultural cleansing, in which the toppling of statues, the censorship of un-PC sitcoms and the cancellation of dissenting voices were presented as blows for progress.

In 2020, freedom, democracy and universalism — the values we at *spiked* hold most dear — were brought under renewed attack. The hard-won gains of the previous few years — the ballot-box revolts that challenged our intolerant, anti-democratic, increasingly identitarian elites — were seemingly cast aside, by a political class drunk on lockdown authoritarianism and a woke set keen to usher in its orthodoxies.

Freedom of speech, above all else, has taken a battering. Big Tech censorship has become increasingly unabashed. British police have taken to investigating YouTubers. And France mourned the murder of Samuel Paty, a teacher beheaded by an Islamist for showing Muhammad cartoons to his students.

This book, bringing together some of *spiked* writers' best pieces from 2020, charts a roughly chronological path through this maddening year. But just as it begins on a note of optimism, with Brexit Day, it ends on one, too: with a US election that turned citizens out in historic numbers, and an unexpectedly close result that showed voters still refuse to do as they're told.

Thank you to all our excellent writers for their contributions to *spiked* this year. And thank you to our readers, whose support has allowed our voice to grow louder even in these bleak times. The next year will still be tough for many. But let's make 2021 the year of the fightback — for freedom, for democracy, and for sanity.

THE MAGNIFICENCE OF BREXIT

BRENDAN O'NEILL

We did it. Against all the odds. Against the barbs and defamations and underhand tactics of a hysterical establishment. Against a Remainer Parliament that had been hell-bent on reversing what we voted for. Against the best efforts of Remainer agitators at home and the bureaucratic machine in Brussels to prevent our democratic voice from being heard.

Against all of this, we did it: we secured the UK's exit from the EU. And now, on Brexit Day, on this day when the Eurosceptic wishes of the British people finally become a reality, let's be frank about what Brexit represents: it is the most significant and stirring political achievement of the postwar period.

As we approach 11pm, the moment at which the UK will no longer be a member of the EU, there is much discussion about what tone we should adopt in our celebrations of Brexit Day. Brexiteer Tory MP Steve Baker is calling for 'magnanimity'. Have a quiet one, at home, so that you don't upset pained Remainers, he suggests.

Remainers, for their part, are furious about all the talk of parties. We're rubbing their noses in it, they say. Everything from the Brexit Day gathering in Parliament Square this evening to the issuing of a commemorative 50p coin is being cited by the establishment's bruised, Remoaning anti-democrats as proof of the vile populist streak in the Brexit movement. London mayor Sadiq Khan is even fretting that tonight's Brexit bashes could give rise to xenophobic hate crimes.

Of course he is. That's how they see us: as a pogrom-in-waiting. As a racist blob. As an unthinking mass driven almost entirely by hatred of the Other. They've been hurling these insults at us, at the millions of men and women who voted for Brexit, for three-and-a-half years now.

But all sides in the Brexit Day discussion are wrong. Timid Brexiteers are wrong to suggest we should play down the significance of this day lest we offend Remainers, and the Brexitphobic wing of the elite is wrong to say these celebrations are a screech of populist arrogance against the defeated side in the referendum. No, the reason this day must be marked — loudly, firmly and colourfully — is because it represents a glorious victory for democracy. What is being celebrated today is the defence of democracy against one of the greatest threats it has faced in modern times.

One of the peculiarities of the Brexit era, and of the contemporary era more broadly, is that very small and very unrepresentative sections of society are in control of the political and moral narrative. So even as 17.4million people, the largest electoral bloc in our history, voted for Brexit, and stood by their vote for Brexit in the face of the most extraordinary campaign of demonisation that I can remember, still the Remainer elites got to write the story of Brexit.

The powers-that-be — from the business elites to more than 70 per cent of MPs to virtually the entire academy and cultural sphere — were pro-Remain. And they used their influence in the worlds of commentary, letters and culture to paint a picture of Brexit as disastrous. As toxic. As fascistic. Or, at best, as very, very difficult to enact. The disjoint between public enthusiasm for Brexit and elite disgust with it was, at times, staggering.

As a consequence, it became incredibly difficult to draw out the historic significance, the magnificence, of Brexit. Even those in public life who supported Brexit, no doubt feeling the pressure of the often furious establishment narrative around Brexit, became defensive. Brexit was manageable, they insisted. It would be okay. 'Get Brexit Done', as the Boris Johnson campaign said in December — a tellingly apologetic slogan that, thankfully, was enough to win the support of vast numbers of Leave voters, but which implicitly played into the denigration of Brexit, the reduction of it to a difficult, pesky task. Hardly anywhere was there an assertion of the historic, epoch-defining nature of Brexit.

So let's do that today. Let's now celebrate the meaningfulness of Brexit. It really cannot be overstated. Brexit is one of the finest acts of democracy in the history of this nation. It ought to take its place in the history books alongside the Levellers' demand for universal male suffrage in the 1640s, and the mass march for democracy on St Peter's Field in Manchester in 1819, and the Chartists' agitation for the right of working-class men to vote in the 1840s, and the civil disobedience of the Suffragettes in the 1910s ...

Because Brexit, and, more importantly, the post-referendum battle to protect Brexit from the anti-democratic elites, shares something incredibly important in common with those democratic leaps forward in British history. Which is that it embodies the patient but determined assertion of ordinary people that they have as much right as the rich and the well-educated to determine the political fate of the nation. That belief in the rights of the people energised the men, women and children on St Peter's Field in 1819, and the women who gathered outside parliament on Black Friday in November 1910, and also the millions of us who voted to leave the EU and take back democratic control. Brexit is in keeping, entirely, with the great democratic struggles of our history.

Brexit did not only entail the British people reprimanding and rejecting the European Union and its anti-democratic ideology, which would have been wonderful enough. Even more importantly than that, Brexit was also a revolt against the *domestic* elites. Against the establishment that pleaded with us to vote Remain in 2016 and which devoted so much of its moral and political energy to sabotaging our vote for Brexit after 2016. Against a political class that, alarmingly, called into question the right to vote itself after the 2016 referendum and openly suggested that this mass vote should be ignored, erased, thrown into the dustbin of history.

This is why the vote for Boris in the 2019 General Election was so significant. That so many 'Red Wall' Labour strongholds fell to the Tories was the clearest sign that the people still wanted Brexit and that the working classes had finally broken from the Labour bureaucracy and asserted their political and moral independence. The December election was the first time in the history of the European Union that a people refused to allow their vote against the EU to be overthrown or stitched up, as tragically happened in Ireland, the Netherlands, France, Greece and elsewhere. Across Europe, under extraordinary pressure from Brussels, Eurosceptic

votes have either been ignored or overridden. Not this time.
The people of Britain voted against the EU and then voted against
the Brussels and British establishments' efforts to crush our vote
and to deny us our democratic rights. This was a genuinely stirring
and determined defence of the ideal of democracy and the meaning
of the vote itself. In response to the most explicit establishment
campaign against democracy in living memory, the British people
said: 'No, no, no.'

If that isn't something to celebrate, I don't know what is. Today,
we should celebrate the British people's defence of democracy.
We should celebrate their perseverance and patience. We should
celebrate the electorate's capacity to think for itself, as captured in
its constant refusal to fall for Project Fear or to heed the desperate
overtures of the Remainer establishment. We should celebrate that
the populist moment, the Europe-wide desire for greater people
power, is not going away anytime soon. And we should celebrate
the seismic shock that Brexit — that is, *us*, the voters — have delivered
to our complacent elites. We have called into question their authority,
their power, and their unilateral right to impose their eccentric values
and managerial tactics on the population at large. That battle isn't
over yet, not by a long shot, but the first victory belongs to the demos.

People fought and died for the right to have a real, impactful
say in political life. And Brexiteers have done those people proud.
I'm celebrating that.

31 JANUARY 2020

THE MYTHS OF MEGXIT

TOM SLATER

First they said Brexit was caused by racism. Now they're saying Megxit was caused by racism.

By 'they', I mean the liberal-left, the people who hate Brexit, hate ordinary people, and have for some reason grown to love our departing royals, Prince Harry and Meghan Markle.

After the Duke and Duchess of Sussex announced that they planned to leave the royal family, but keep their royal titles and most of their royal income, commentators have closed ranks around the couple, like some woke version of the Queen's Guard.

They have chastised anyone outraged by the staggering entitlement shown by the Sussexes, who have essentially said that they want the status but none of the responsibilities of monarchy. They insist that the poor couple has been driven out by racism.

British author Afua Hirsch, writing in the *New York Times*, decries the 'racist treatment of Meghan' in the press. She says it is hardly a surprise that Markle has walked away from a nation with a prime minister 'whose track record includes overtly racist statements' and a 'Brexit project linked to native nationalism'.

Of course, Boris Johnson has no such track record and the only people linking Brexit to native nationalism are upper-crust Remainers like Hirsch. But no matter. Why let reality spoil the narrative?

These claims made about the 'racist' treatment of Meghan at the hands of the British tabloids are incredibly thin. The same non-examples are recycled over and over again. You'll have seen them quoted (out of context) a thousand times.

There's a *Daily Mail* piece from 2016, when Harry and Meghan were first dating, that said she was '(almost) straight outta Compton' (at the time Markle's mother lived in nearby Crenshaw, LA). Hirsch says this was an attempt to link Meghan with 'racialised forms of crime' – that is, gangs.

That's one hell of a reach. The piece was clearly just playing on the difference in Harry and Meghan's social backgrounds. If Harry had been dating a white working-class woman from Moss Side, I dare say the *Mail* would have done something similarly silly.

Another favourite is that weird throwaway line Rachel Johnson wrote, in a laudatory piece on Markle, about the mixed-race American actress bringing some 'rich and exotic DNA' to the pale Windsor bloodline. That's more cringey than racist.

Several pieces have even cited a single phrase in a Sarah Vine column – she said she had a 'niggling worry' about the royal couple's engagement photo – as a bigoted dog whistle. Which is, quite frankly, mental. Such is the lack of actual examples of the press being racist towards Meghan.

The only leg this argument has left to stand on is that the sheer volume of criticism sent Markle's way was disproportionate, and racism is the only explanation for it. It's an argument that has the advantage of being based purely on unverifiable speculation and imputing motives. But it's also, obviously, bollocks.

When the couple first got together the coverage was pretty much gushing across the board. It was only when Meghan and Harry started on their various virtue-signalling crusades – like jetting around to lecture on climate change – that people's backs went up.

That the couple had already been beefing with the press probably didn't help either. In 2016, way before Meghan became such a key figure in our culture wars, Harry issued a remarkable statement rebuking journalists for the 'racial undertones' of their pieces.

That these privileged royals, kept in the lap of luxury at tax-payers' expense, began to develop a deep-seated victim complex only deepened the resentment towards them. In 2019, Meghan told ITV that public life was a 'struggle', and that she was shocked that 'not many people have asked if I'm okay'. Poor princess.

This picture of privilege is who the liberal-left has spent the best part of three years defending. Even supposed republicans have – after a bit of anti-royal throat-clearing – defended Harry and Meghan to the hilt and helped construct this absurd narrative that they are the victims of establishment racism.

But this says far more about the prejudices of metropolitan commentators than it does about the tabloid press. That they routinely situate Meghan's supposed mistreatment in Brexit Britain is no coincidence. They think of Britain as a foul place, full of foul people, brainwashed by foul newspapers to hate the wonderful Duchess of Sussex and the obviously brilliant European Union.

What the liberal elites' nasty case of Meghanmania has shown us is that, for all their posturing against right-wingers, monarchy and the old aristocracy, they're completely comfortable with the plebs being led and instructed and hectored by our betters.

They would just rather it was woke people doing it. People like Harry and Meghan.

10 JANUARY 2020

GREENS VS DEMOCRACY

TIM BLACK

One week, it's that old Malthusian, David Attenborough, telling us 'the moment of crisis has come'. The next it's that young Malthusian, Greta Thunberg, telling us 'our house is still on fire' and 'inaction is fuelling the flames'.

Both express the key elements of today's environmentalist script. The shrill tone. The end-is-nigh urgency. The act-now-or-else command. And underwriting this script is the core idea of contemporary environmentalism – namely, the climate emergency. This is the idea that so imminent and existential is the threat of climate change that world leaders need to act as if they are at war. They need to declare a state of emergency. There's no time for deliberation or debate anymore, because, well, 'our house is on fire'. In this state of emergency, all civil liberties and democratic freedoms can be suspended. All dissent and debate silenced. Only then will the authorities, using all force necessary, be able to do what needs to be done to protect us from the enemy. It just so happens that this enemy is us, and our all-consuming passions.

This wartime analogy has long lurked on the fringes of the environmentalist movement. It crops up, for instance, in James Lovelock's 2009 broadside, *The Vanishing Face of Gaia*. He writes that surviving climate change 'may require, as in war, the suspension of democratic government for the duration of the survival emergency'.

But only now has it entered the mainstream. So, in May 2019, the *Guardian* revised its style guide, stating that 'instead of "climate change", the preferred terms are "climate emergency, crisis or break-down"'. That same month, the UK became the first nation state to

declare a climate emergency, days after similar declarations from
Scotland and Wales. In June, New York City became the world's
largest city to declare a climate emergency. And then, in November,
the European Parliament did likewise for the EU. Little wonder
Oxford Dictionaries made 'climate emergency' its word of the year.

Not everyone has been quite as keen to embrace the emergency
rhetoric. In November, a few MEPs from the European Parliament's
largest bloc, the European People's Party, struck a note of caution
amid the EU's clamour for a declaration of climate emergency.
They were worried that the language was just a little too redolent
of Nazi-era Germany.

Which is understandable. The emergency Reichstag Fire Decree,
issued on 28 February 1933 after the German parliamentary building
had been burnt down, permitted the suspension of the democratic
aspects of the soon-to-disappear Weimar Republic, and legally
sanctioned the Nazis' suppression and persecution of political
opponents. That, after all, is what states of emergency tend to entail:
a clampdown on civil and democratic freedom in the interests of
preserving the state against a perceived existential threat. And that
is what the climate emergency entails, too.

All this raises a few questions. Given the unpleasant, brown-shirted
whiff steaming off the idea of a climate emergency, why are political
and cultural elites in the EU, the UK and the US so willing to embrace
it? And, more pertinently, why now?

It cannot be fully explained by reference to the state of the
environment, no matter how devastating the Australian bushfires
or destructive the floods in northern England. For there is always
more to environmentalism than environmental challenges. And
the 'more' in this case is the seismic shift in the post-2016 political
landscape. It is a landscape in which Western elites find themselves
mortally threatened not so much by climate change as by those
they can blame for it – the people. And this is precisely why climate
change has resurged as an issue over the past few years, and why
the profoundly anti-democratic idea of a climate emergency lies at
its heart. Because it is being mobilised against the populist threat.

The shift in tone of the climate-change issue is marked. When
environmentalism last enjoyed its moment in the blazing sun, in
the mid-2000s, it was also pushing a catastrophist narrative. It could

hardly have been otherwise, given its anti-Enlightenment, Malthusian origins. But the approach was condescendingly scientistic, rather than shrill and panic-stricken. The truth was 'inconvenient', rather than compelling. An Intergovernmental Panel on Climate Change report would offer a 'very likely' range of future scenarios, rather than declare an emergency. But then environmentalism preached to estranged, often understandably bored electorates, rather than recalcitrant, restive ones.

This patronising, scientistic tone reflected environmentalism's political, ideological function, as a legitimising gloss painted on to Western political elites' administration of things. It was the handmaiden of technocracy and managerialism. It allowed post-Cold War elites to disavow modernity, justify long-term economic stagnation, and provide their Third Way governance with a semblance of purpose.

The financial crash and subsequent economic crisis was to sideline environmentalism. From 2008 onwards, justifying economic stagnation no longer needed a green dressing. It could become, as 'austerity', a policy and ideology in its own right. Hence, from the UK to the crisis-ridden eurozone, politicians of all stripes now talked of fiscal responsibility, of cutting back and consuming less.

2016 changed everything. The populist challenge to the political classes of Europe and the US, which had been stirring for a while, erupted. And environmentalism resurged in response. It had always served as a way of managing the public, of justifying the political class's mode of governance. Now it could serve as a way of quelling the populist challenge. Of diminishing people's democratic aspirations. Of suppressing the rejection of technocracy and managerialism. After all, what is politics beside the climate emergency?

Climate activists, a uniformly bourgeois bunch as opposed to Brexit as they are to Trump voters, have rallied. *Rising Up!*, the group that was to launch Extinction Rebellion in 2018, staged its first 'action' in November 2016. And the teachers' pets of the Climate Strike movement began theirs in the summer of 2018.

Sometimes they have positioned themselves explicitly against Brexit or Trump. But often they don't need to. Their climate-emergency message does the job implicitly, functioning, as it does, as an all-purpose means to diminish and even suppress the democratic ambitions of the revolting masses.

Little wonder, then, that environmentalism is so central to the preservation of the status quo today. The climate emergency is the elites' response to the populist challenge. It represents the suspension of people's democratic aspirations. The suspension of politics. But, as has been demonstrated ever since 2016, the populist challenge resists suspension.

24 JANUARY 2020

THE LEFT'S PROBLEM WITH BRITISH INDIANS

RAKIB EHSAN

Boris Johnson's cabinet now includes four politicians of Indian descent. Priti Patel remains as home secretary and three British Indians have been appointed in new roles. Rishi Sunak is now chancellor of the exchequer, promoted in spectacular fashion following Sajid Javid's resignation. Indian-born Alok Sharma has replaced Andrea Leadsom as business and energy secretary. And Suella Braverman has replaced Geoffrey Cox as attorney general and is now the government's top lawyer.

These are interesting developments in an administration that has been accused by its more hysterical critics of being essentially ethno-nationalist. Indeed, the Conservative Party's relationship with British Indians – an admittedly diverse group in terms of migratory background and religious affiliation – is one of the more interesting developments of recent times. Traditionally, British Indians provided the Labour Party with high levels of electoral support – in part due to the party's passage of race-relations legislation and its broader reputation for fighting racism.

But things have changed. Today, British Indians are one of the highest-earning ethnic groups in Britain, earning more on average per hour than the white British majority. British Indians are renowned for their entrepreneurial spirit and are generally not instinctive supporters of the high-tax, large-spend economic policies associated with Labour. Like most Brits, many British Indians are far from impressed with Labour's – particularly Jeremy Corbyn's – ties with Islamist organisations, and the party's reluctance to discuss the terror threat posed by Islamist extremism.

Support for Labour among British Pakistani and British Bangladeshi Muslims has remained exceptionally high over the past few General Elections. But among British Indians, support for the Conservatives has steadily grown.

The 2019 General Election showed a further fraying of the relationship between Labour and British Indians. In Harrow East – a west London seat with a sizeable Indian-origin population – Labour fell some way behind. Conservative MP Bob Blackman increased his vote share by five percentage points. Leicester has the second-largest Indian-born population in Britain. In the last election, in Leicester West and Leicester East, Labour's vote share dropped by 11 and 16 percentage points respectively.

The fact that British Indians have been so successful and have integrated into society should be celebrated by the left. Here is a story of migrants, refugees and their descendants making notable contributions to British public life – in business, politics, media, entertainment, sport and more.

However, the identitarian left is much more interested in keeping ethnic minorities locked into a perpetual state of victimhood. The values of personal responsibility, individual initiative and self-sufficiency, which run deep in British Indian communities, challenge the left's grievance-driven narratives. The fact that British Indians have managed to thrive also calls the widespread notion of 'white privilege' into question.

A good number of British Indians hold culturally conservative views, which are fundamentally at odds with left-wing cosmopolitanism, particularly on issues such as immigration and integration. Indians are also the most pro-Brexit of the UK's non-white ethnic groups.

Politicians of Indian heritage are a growing force in high-level Tory politics, and this has made them a target for the left. This often spills over into racial slurs. British Indian Conservative politicians have effectively been branded Uncle Toms and race traitors. One left-wing writer described them as 'turncoats of colour'. Home secretary Priti Patel has been accused of having 'internalised whiteness' and a 'Raj complex'. In a pathetic hit piece, the *Guardian* – the bastion of chattering-class intolerance – highlighted Suella Braverman's membership of a Buddhist sect, which it said could 'raise questions' about 'her judgement as the government's senior legal expert'. No doubt the left would be quick to call out such slurs and innuendos if they were directed at others.

The British left today refuses to acknowledge the role of individual initiative and personal success, appears soft on issues from terrorism to crime, and treats minorities who do not fit its victim narrative as traitors. No wonder British Indians are looking elsewhere.

20 FEBRUARY 2020

PUT IT AWAY, LOVE

JULIE BURCHILL

No one could accuse me of not liking vaginas; I'm especially keen on mine. I don't sit around staring at it the way I did when I was a youngster, like it was suddenly going to speak up and reveal the secret of life, but I could still pick it out in a police line-up. Though I vastly prefer male genitalia (the conjuring-trick aspect never fails to amaze me), it certainly wasn't vaginas that put me off being a lesbian way back when I tried it on for size for six months — it was the crying.

Nevertheless, even a broad-minded broad such as myself must admit to perplexity and just a little distaste about the mingemania currently sweeping the Western world. It's one thing to free women from shame; it's another entirely to do as the Fanny Fanclub is doing, lecturing us endlessly that we don't talk about our vaginas enough.

There's a *Happy Vagina* podcast, and a website with the unfortunate name of OMGyes, teaching women how to have orgasms — which is surely as superfluous as teaching people how to chew. Of course, where there's woke brass there's celebrities. Emma Watson smugged of OMGyes, 'It's an expensive subscription but it's worth it'.

And then of course there's Croesus of Crank turned Onassis of Onanism, Gwyneth Paltrow, who can't stand to think there's one crotch in Christendom that she hasn't squeezed some cash out of. Paltrow made headlines in 2015 when, through her lifestyle brand Goop, she promoted the vaginal steamer: 'You sit on what is essentially a mini-throne, and a combination of infrared and mugwort steam cleanses your uterus.' If that didn't clean you out, her website also sold a $15,000 24-carat gold-plated dildo. (Surely no one that rich can be that lonely?)

In 2018, Paltrow was fined $145,000 for making unscientific claims about the effectiveness of vaginal jade eggs, which Goop claimed could 'balance hormones, regulate menstrual cycles, prevent uterine prolapse, and increase bladder control'. Undeterred, she has continued to milk this golden gynaecological goose by issuing a scented candle called 'This Smells Like My Vagina' and promoting her new Netflix show by appearing in front of a vagina made of flowers.

If ever there was a woman who made me want to yell 'Put it away!', it's this one. Though Madonna would come a close second; the unstoppable sexagenarian recently told an audience at the London Palladium that she had 'a musical vagina'; what a shame she hasn't acquired a musical voice over the course of her long and discordant career.

It's not just established stars who are standing up to be counted for the sheer molten miracle of possessing genitals, but also the aspiring showbiz kids. Grace Campbell, comedian daughter of Alastair, recently tweeted her new vagina necklace, which she wears proudly as part of a campaigning group called 'The Pink Protest'. This group is actually worthwhile, lobbying as it does to beef up the law on the horror of female genital mutilation. But then they have to go and spoil it all by running a campaign called – excuse my French – #GirlsWankToo, which sets out to demystify the 'taboo' that surrounds female masturbation.

I'm no prude, but if I needed to see illustrations of women riding pink dildos on Instagram in order to give myself permission to touch myself, I'd probably have decided it wasn't for me and kept my hands busy by taking up sampler sewing.

Once again, there are genuine problems in this delicate area that every responsible citizen needs to be aware of. According to the NHS, even voluntary cosmetic labiaplasty puts women at risk of scarring and reduced sensitivity, yet it is increasing year on year. The Eve Appeal, which focuses on female cancers, has concluded that there is 'a dangerous knowledge gap' in women's understanding of their own anatomy.

It also found that 65 per cent of women aged 16 to 25 have a problem using the word 'vagina', while nearly 40 per cent say they resort to using code names such as 'lady parts' to discuss gynaecological health. I know this is meant to be A Bad Thing, but to be fair most of us have pet names for things we love; if my husband ever calls me 'Julie' I know I'm in trouble.

Looking up the dirty bits in books is always a popular teenage pastime, so I do approve of the number of explicitly biological books being published at the moment, which cut out all the searching for today's fortunate youth. But on closer examination, with so much emphasis being put on all the misery reproductive organs can cause, are we not in danger of turning our randy island race into facsimiles of those poor Japanese teens who would rather stay in their bedrooms playing videogames than do the dirty deed?

A welcome exception is the brisk if somewhat insensitively named *The Vagina Bible*, by the splendid American gynaecologist, Dr Jen Gunter. In the name of sisterhood I shouldn't say this, but her recent radio slam dunk of what Paltrow has been peddling was sublime.

We stray into the realms of the ridiculous, however, when we survey some of the stupid v-related gifts on sale today: a crocheted tampon keyring, enamel vagina badges, a notebook bearing the front-cover inscription 'YOU MAKE ME AND MY VAGINA SO HAPPY', and of course that reliable indicator of whether or not grown adults should have their right to vote removed – colouring books.

Like vibrators disguised to look like bath playthings, I find there's something both icky and sinister here that seeks to infantilise sex. It *is* a dirty business – if you do it properly – and at a time when we are finally conscious of the repulsive level of paedophilia that the patriarchy has spawned, mixing sex up with toys seems shady, to say the least.

Of course gynophobia exists – whole religions revolve around it. I'm just rather suspicious that the sort of woke handmaidens who you see bigging up their vaginas by wearing pink pussy hats on anti-Trump marches will before long be hijabing up as another way of laughably defying toxic masculinity. Where's the logic in yelling about sexual pride when you're embracing a religion in which women are treated like a cross between children and domestic animals?

And in another clash of interests, these sorts of sob sisters often slander their fellow feminists as TERFS in order to suck up to the trans lobby, which would like to see the female orifice reduced to the insulting phrase 'front hole'. Indeed, the Vagina Museum – which opened in 2019 – promises to 'challenge heteronormative and cisnormative behaviour' and 'promote intersectional, feminist and trans-inclusive values'. If part of this challenge is insisting that the ridiculous openings fashioned during sex-change operations are actual vaginas, one might as well showcase a performance by the Black and White Minstrels as part of Black History Month.

The museum's curator, Sarah Creed, told the *Guardian*: 'We are an LGBTQ+ ally and an intersex ally ... intersex and trans individuals are not represented at all in this narrative. We are looking at how we can engage all people. I want cis heterosexual men to come here and feel it is a space for them to come and learn.'

Tellingly, it has applied to Camden Council for a liquor licence so that the museum can 'survive financially'. But somehow, hordes of drunken men leering at strangers' vaginas sounds wearisomely familiar and contemptible rather than thrillingly new and challenging. Liquor licence or not, I think I'll give it a miss – as someone said of *The Vagina Monologues*, 'If I want to see hundreds of people yelling the c-word, I can go to a football match'.

It would be a shame if, having protested for so long that women are more than their sex organs, we came to elevate them above all our other parts – especially our brains.

2 MARCH 2020

DISSENT IN A TIME OF COVID

BRENDAN O'NEILL

Two nasty ailments have gripped Britain. The first is Covid-19.
The second is intolerance of dissent. The authoritarian instincts of
the chattering classes have been on full display in this crisis. You can
see it in their daily pleas for Boris Johnson to turn the UK into a police
state. You can see it in their sneering at people who visit parks or
take a walk on a beachfront. And you can see it most disturbingly in
their implacable rage against anyone who deviates from the Covid-19
script and asks if shutting down society really is the right thing to
do. Like medieval scolds, they brand such people dangerous, insane,
a virus, accessories to manslaughter. 'Shut them down!', they cry,
thinking they are signalling their concern for the public's health
when really they are advertising their profound contempt for
freedom of thought and critical debate.

   In an emergency, freedom of speech doesn't stop being important.
It becomes more important. The vast majority of people accept there
will be restrictions on their everyday freedoms in the next few months.
They know they won't be able to socialise very much and will have
to stay indoors for long periods of time. We accept this because, in
contradiction of the anti-masses hatred coming from the media elites
at the moment, who are fuming over photographs of what they view
as thick, ignorant scum walking in parks, people actually have a
strong sense of social solidarity. They are concerned for the health
of their friends, families, community and society. They accept
restrictions to that end. But even in a moment like this there should
be not a single restriction on freedom of speech. The right to dissent

from the middle-class apocalypticism enveloping the Covid-19 crisis is the most important liberty right now.

And it's a liberty under threat. The speed with which questioning extreme responses to Covid-19 has become tantamount to a speechcrime is alarming. I got a taste of it when I found myself in the eye of a storm over a piece I wrote questioning the wisdom of closing pubs. Peter Hitchens did too, after he wrote a piece questioning the shutdown of society. Others who have wondered out loud if the freezing of social and economic life is the right response to this new virus have been hounded, shamed, reported to the Silicon Valley authorities. Labour MP David Lammy calls us insane and dangerous and says our words should be unpublished. Unpersoning will be next. Questioning the lockdown will see you blacklisted from polite society.

How swiftly we become McCarthyites. How naturally intolerance comes to that section of society that thinks it knows best. Partly, of course, this is always its default mode. As we know from the past couple of decades of social shaming, No Platforming and outright state assaults against people who are deemed to hold hateful or wrongthink views, the new elites are not exactly friends of freedom of speech. But the rising tide of Covid-19 censoriousness also suggests that these people think that when things get serious, when society faces a genuine threat, then freedom of speech becomes a negotiable commodity. Words potentially become dangerous. Bad ideas can lead to loss of life. So police speech, shame the dissenters, silence the 'virus' of incorrect thought. This is as wrong as it is possible for someone to be. It is precisely moments like this that show why freedom of speech is the most important value in a civilised, democratic society.

Right now, our societies are doing something historically unprecedented. They are asking us to change our lives in ways that would have been unimaginable just a couple of weeks ago. Some European societies have completely shut down. This week the UK will likely introduce a Coronavirus Bill that will give our government extraordinary power over individuals and public space. The right to question this is essential, for two reasons. First, because we should *never* feel comfortable with restrictions on freedom.

Even if we accept them as short-term measures in a mass act of social solidarity to protect life, they should still make us bristle and balk and constantly ask questions: 'Why is this necessary? When will it end?'

And the second reason freedom of speech becomes even more important in a crisis is because of one of the key things that freedom of speech does – it encourages intellectual humility. Freedom of speech is the means through which all of us entertain the possibility that we are wrong. The great service of freedom of speech is that it helps us question ourselves. The unfettered existence of all kinds of interesting, challenging, strange and offensive views is the great and essential guard against our own tendencies to dogma. It invites rethinking, re-evaluation. It gives us that great liberty: the liberty to change our minds.

Dogma, in contrast, does the opposite. Dogma emerges where people shield themselves, normally courtesy of censorship, from the thoughts and questions and criticisms of others. Forcefielding oneself and one's ideas from criticism gives rise to lazy, sclerotic thinking. It nurtures orthodoxies and blind beliefs, ideologies that are cleaved to not because their worth and substance have been properly tested through rigorous public debate, but because we *just know* they are right. Doing that in normal times is bad enough. Doing that in a time of unprecedented crisis is lethal. It means this: society might go down a route that is wrong. I'm not saying it is wrong. But shouldn't we entertain the possibility that it is? Shouldn't we nurture the conditions of freedom in which the potential wrongness of what we are doing could be exposed? Shouldn't we be humble rather than dogmatic about the overhaul of modern life, and open to the possibility that it is a mistake?

I want to hear from dissenters who think that what we are doing is wrong. Their voices are immeasurably important right now. They will protect us from the disease of dogma. I want to hear from people like David L Katz, founding director of the Yale-Griffin Prevention Research Center, who says the lockdown might be a mistake; that this 'near total meltdown of normal life – schools and businesses closed, gatherings banned – [might be] long-lasting and calamitous, possibly graver than the direct toll of the virus itself'. I want to hear from those, like Katz, who are asking if the lockdown itself could actually help to spread the disease, for example by closing colleges and schools and sending 'young people of indeterminate infectious status ... to huddle with their families'.

I want to hear from people like Professor Michael T Osterholm, director of the Center for Infectious Disease Research and Policy at the University of Minnesota, who says 'a national lockdown is no cure'. Who says we must urgently 'consider the effect of shutting down offices, schools, transportation systems, restaurants, hotels, stores, theatres, concert halls, sporting events and other venues indefinitely and leaving all of their workers unemployed and on the public dole'. 'The likely result', he says, 'would be not just a depression but a complete economic breakdown'.

I want to hear from people like Gerd Gigerenzer, director of the Harding Center for Risk Literacy at the Max Planck Institute for Human Development in Berlin, who reminds us that apocalyptic predictions were made about earlier viral diseases and they did not come true. Who reminds us that the UK government predicted that 65,000 Brits would die from swine flu in 2009, but actually fewer than 500 died. Who says there are dangers both to underreaction *and* overreaction to Covid-19, and that our society must learn to live with this uncertainty.

I want to hear from these voices because they can help to hold at bay the desire for unflinching certainty and dogmatic responses in the face of Covid-19, neither of which are helpful, and both of which could end up causing as much harm to society and our wellbeing as the disease itself. The instinct to demonise and shut down anyone who says we are overreacting to Covid-19 is not only irritatingly censorious and anti-intellectual — it is potentially dangerous, too, since it will erase those opinions that are holding out the possibility that what we are doing is wrong. 'Am I wrong?' has never been a more important question to ask ourselves. And freedom of speech is the thing that makes that question possible, makes it meaningful, and gives it the extraordinary power to protect society from good intentions that might have terrible consequences.

23 MARCH 2020

KEIR STARMER'S UNBEARABLE NOTHINGNESS

TOM SLATER

Say what you like about Keir Starmer, the newly elected leader of the Labour Party, he's got a great head of hair for a man in his late fifties. In his pre-recorded winner's speech, released just after it was announced that he had run away with the leadership race by winning 56 per cent of the vote, it was hard not to admire that somewhat oddly sculpted quiff, not least because, as is often the case with Starmer, it was genuinely difficult to follow what he was saying.

Listening to Starmer speak feels like slowly drowning in blancmange. It's not that what he's saying is incoherent, or rambly. Far from it. Everything this former barrister says feels carefully, even overly, considered. It's just that what he says is kind of nothingy, replete with platitudes and wispy, high-minded rhetoric that evaporates upon contact with your brain. Pair it with his negative charisma and it's a remarkably numbing combination.

His speech opened on the coronavirus crisis before hammering the message of his campaign – that he will lead Labour into government while not ditching the 'radicalism' of the Corbyn era. It was all completely lifeless, ending on the anti-climactic lines: 'I will lead this great party into a new era, with confidence and with hope. So that when the time comes, we can serve our country again in government.' How the earth moved.

There is a point in all this. Namely, that Starmer's politics are as empty as his rhetoric. His campaign, which brought on board people from the right and left of the party, was an exercise in hedging. He paid lip service to socialism and radicalism, keen to keep the Corbynite membership on side. But he did so in a way that was entirely devoid of substance, reducing socialism in one op-ed to a desire to 'stand up for the powerless against the powerful'.

Political journalists have been dispatched to dredge through his past to get some idea of what he believes. That such archaeology is necessary is perhaps telling. Piece after piece tells stories of his younger days writing for obscure Trotskyist journals and his legal work defending striking workers and environmentalists. But the real picture that emerges is, in the words of one profiler, of a creature of the 'liberal legal technocracy'.

Starmer, the former director of public prosecutions, seems to put store not in politics or ideology, but in process, institutions and legalism. Which is probably why he is so keen on the European Union. Indeed, that the architect of Labour's second-referendum policy, which basically handed many working-class Leave voters to the Tories, is now charged with winning back the party's old heartlands is too stupid for words.

What Starmer heralds is a return to dry managerialism, and in this he is effectively surrendering any sense of dynamism to the Tories. The remarkable things it has been forced to do in response to coronavirus aside, the Johnson regime is not particularly radical – it has been nicely summed up as 'Blairism plus Brexit'. But at least it has managed to speak to the new populist, democratic mood sparked by the referendum.

Now, the supposed radicalism of the Corbyn era is often overstated. At most it aspired to a knackered old model of state socialism. It was also a project riddled with fatal contradictions. It was a party 'for the many' that wanted to overturn the votes of 17.4million people; a 'socialist' party that wanted desperately to stay in the neoliberal EU. That Starmer has so easily seized Corbyn's Labour shows how thin an ideology Corbynism always was.

But there's no doubt that Starmer's victory marks a formal retreat into the kind of bloodless technocracy that has drained social-democratic parties across the West of both their substance and their electoral base. The Covid-19 crisis has of course changed everything. Who knows what will happen at the next election. But it's hard to see how Sir Keir could possibly return this alleged party of the working class to former glories. Great hair, though.

4 APRIL 2020

DON'T GIVE IN TO FEAR

BRENDAN O'NEILL

A sense of dread has descended on Britain. It is palpable. This once productive, busy, culturally alive nation has, like many others, become hushed and atomised over the past two weeks. Every suburb is a ghost town. Trips to the pub or cinema are becoming distant memories, from the old era, the era of BC: Before Coronavirus. Our only connection with each other is in the *Blankety Blank*-style square boxes of a Zoom chat – social life reduced to a stilted, awkward gameshow-like exchange of quarantine stories, tips to avoid getting fat, and updates on how much booze we're all drinking. (Lots, is the answer. National sales are up by more than 20 per cent.)

And now, into these strange, apocalyptic rituals that pass for life in Covid-hit Britain, comes the news that the PM himself is in intensive care with the blasted virus. Yes, the man who was leading the fight against the virus has been laid low by the virus. Hopefully not for long. There is widespread concern and support for Boris Johnson. The nation is willing him to get well, willing him back to the political frontline. But there is no question that the absence of the man who was so enthusiastically elected just four months ago has added to the sense of foreboding, to a feeling across the nation that life and politics and freedom as we knew them fell apart very quickly, and may be difficult to repair.

Yes, it isn't all bad news. The social solidarity we have seen in recent weeks has been inspiring. Neighbours who might never have spoken to each other before are now pulling together to shop for old people and deliver medicines to the vulnerable. More than 700,000 people volunteered to assist the NHS. The queen's positive message to the nation – surely her best ever, this republican believes – captured many people's optimistic belief that Britain will get through this and 'we will meet again'. But even for all of that, life has become strange and difficult, and at times like this it is really important to take stock, to stay reasoned and, most crucially of all, to refuse to let fear in.

Fear is the insatiable beast that feeds on our worries and uncertainties. Most of us are refusing to feed the monster, but sadly the same cannot be said for other sections of society. The media, in particular, provide hearty meals to the culture of fear every day, with their ceaseless, often context-free horror stories about the wall of death Covid has built. I'm sure many people are switching off, for the good of their health. On the internet, influential dystopian millennials share graphs and stories that are expressly designed to exaggerate the already severe impact of Covid-19. Some almost seem to relish Covid's grip on the nation, at least to the extent that it allows them to say 'I told you so' about Tory Britain or late-stage capitalism. The virus becomes a stand-in for political conviction, the grisly hope being that this virus will do what political campaigns have failed to do: shame the Tories and make the case for state socialism. Fear becomes a political tool.

Most of us are resisting fear. We know it does no good. Getting by in a lockdown becomes that bit more difficult if your mind is occupied by fear. It brings to mind the words of CS Lewis on fear of the atomic bomb. 'The first action to be taken is to pull ourselves together', he said. Just stop thinking about the bomb, was Lewis's advice to mid-20th-century Westerners: 'They may break our bodies ... but they need not dominate our minds.' I feel similarly about Covid-19. It will break some bodies (and everything must be done to ensure it is as few bodies as possible). But it shouldn't occupy our every waking thought. It is causing enough destruction as it is without also setting up camp in our hearts and minds. Fear of Covid-19 is its own virus, a virus that attacks our optimism and self-belief, which is why we are right to turn off the TV, push aside the more panic-stricken newspapers, and just do what we can in a lockdown: talk to family and friends, help the less fortunate, go for walks, eat, drink, watch *Tiger King*. All of these are small acts of resistance against the stalking culture of fear.

And this is why Boris's illness matters, and why it matters that he gets well. It matters first and foremost because he is a human being — a father, a son, a brother, a friend. Every effort should be made to cheer and steer him to good health, as should be done with regards to everyone who gets ill with the virus, whether they are 19 or 90. But it also matters because of what Boris represents. It isn't only that he is leader of the governing party and one of the most popularly elected prime ministers of modern times. There is also the question of what the massive outpouring of democratic support for Boris in December spoke to: a widespread revolt *against the politics of fear*. Millions of people voted for Boris and his simple message of 'Get Brexit Done' in open defiance of three-and-a-half years of Project Fear, which told them that the thing they wanted would ruin the nation and ruin their lives. They resisted this baleful message and essentially said: 'We have more faith in ourselves and our nation than you do. We aren't afraid to take a political risk.'

One of the reasons Boris's victory felt so heartening — even to those of us who are far from natural Conservatives — is because it was a rebellion against the doom-laden overtures and dire warnings of our political and media elites, whose only weapon against our political vision was *fear*. They sought to scare us into changing our minds and into giving up on the political step we wanted to take. But they failed. We refused to let fear in. We refused, to borrow from Lewis, to let them dominate our minds. We drew from the well of national spirit and political confidence — the same well the queen has latterly tapped into — to say: 'Let's do this. We will succeed.' Boris was the beneficiary of this, of the people-made culture of *anti-fear*. He owes his political position and his name in the history books to the British masses' stirring refusal to cave in to fear and instead to believe in themselves and in each other.

That's the tragic irony of Boris's current illness. The man we democratically chose to face down fear and break away from the old, exhausted status quo is now stymied by physical malaise. And there is a serious risk in these circumstances that the things Boris was charged with pushing back against — the politics of fear and also the culture of technocracy — could creep back into public life. No, Boris did not single-handedly hold those two destructive, anti-democratic trends at bay, but he is acutely aware that that is what we, the public, tasked him with doing. There's a possibility that the creeping sense of dread and political disarray in Covid-hit Britain could unwind the hugely positive gains of democracy and confidence the people of Britain made in recent years.

But we mustn't let it. Even as society remains shut down and the virus continues to spread, we have to maintain the culture of anti-fear that we developed as a people over the past four years. 'The only thing we have to fear is fear itself', Franklin D Roosevelt famously said: 'Nameless, unreasoning, unjustified terror which paralyses needed efforts to convert retreat into advance.' We have already rejected that outlook, very recently, and now we must do so again. Reject fear, engage with our communities, and retain the defiant optimism and collective confidence that fuelled the democratic life of this nation over the past four years. People are willing Boris to get well because they want Britain to get well, and they want their grand plans for the nation to be realised. They will be, soon.

7 APRIL 2020

THERE IS NO SUCH THING AS THE SCIENCE

ROB LYONS

According to David Blunkett, a former senior cabinet minister in Tony Blair's governments, attempts to have a blanket lockdown on the over-70s are discriminatory. He believes that the current 'shielding' rules are too crude and need to be more nuanced. Whatever the merits of his ideas, his comments on the scientific advice that the government is receiving are interesting.

Speaking on BBC Radio 4's *The World at One* at the end of April, Blunkett argued that the Scientific Advisory Group for Emergencies (SAGE) has a problem. Drawing on Matthew Syed's book, *Rebel Ideas*, he said that 'major mistakes in the recent past have been made by people of similar ilk, similar ideas, similar background, similar thinking being considered the only experts that you could draw down on. And I'd like RAGE – a Recovery Advisory Group – that had a very much broader swathe of advice and expertise to draw down on.'

The danger of listening to a small pool of experts with orthodox thinking was also pointed to by a former chief scientific adviser, Sir David King. Reacting to reports that Boris Johnson's senior adviser, Dominic Cummings, may have pushed SAGE to back the current lockdown, King told *Bloomberg*: 'There is a herd instinct in all of us – we call it groupthink. It is possible that a group is influenced by a particularly influential person.'

Other leading scientific figures have criticised the idea that the government's policies are based on science. Professor Devi Sridhar, chair of global public health at the University of Edinburgh, told the *Guardian*: 'As a scientist, I hope I never again hear the phrase "based on the best science and evidence" spoken by a politician. This phrase has become basically meaningless and used to explain anything and everything.'

The same article quotes Professor Mark Woolhouse, an infectious-diseases epidemiologist at the University of Edinburgh: 'I do think scientific advice is driven far too much by epidemiology – and I'm an epidemiologist. What we're not talking about in the same formal, quantitative way are the economic costs, the social costs, the psychological costs of being under lockdown. I understand that the government is being advised by economists, psychiatrists and others, but we're not seeing what that science is telling them. I find that very puzzling.'

All these comments and more point to one of the most striking aspects of the Covid-19 crisis. For many years now, politicians – largely bereft of any wider purpose or philosophical principle – have claimed that they are pursuing 'evidence-based policy' and being 'led by The Science'. In reality, science is a process of trying to draw together tentative conclusions driven by experiment and observation. Claiming authority from The Science – as if there were a grand tome you could simply open up to find the correct answer – is just wrong.

As Professor Brian Cox told the BBC's Andrew Marr recently: 'There's no such thing as The Science, which is a key lesson. If you hear a politician say "we're following The Science", then what that means is they don't really understand what science is. There isn't such a thing as The Science. Science is a mindset.'

With widely publicised disagreements about everything from computer models to the use of face masks, it is clear that we need to move beyond the idea that we can rely on scientists coming to a cosy consensus. Science works – at its best – through the accumulation of evidence, an openness to new theories, and a willingness to challenge and be challenged.

It's great that these principles are being restated. Funnily enough, though, this wasn't the reaction we saw over Michael Gove's much-half-quoted comment during the EU referendum – that the public has 'had enough of experts'. (In fact, he said: 'I think the people of this country have had enough of experts from organisations with acronyms saying they know what is best, and getting it consistently wrong.') The trouble with politicians, we were told by Remain-supporting types, is that they don't listen to the cool, rational views of experts nearly enough. Now that it seems that experts might be blamed for the deaths of tens of thousands of people, the expertise cheerleaders are reversing out of that position, pronto.

Actually, the public never gave up on experts. We're only too happy to find out about the latest scientific understanding of the virus, how soon we might have a treatment or a vaccine, and so on. What some have taken issue with is the politicisation of expertise. An unholy alliance of politicians and a selected band of experts, whose views suit the current needs of government, have often in recent years told us what 'The Science says' and urged critics to just shut up — over issues from passive smoking to climate change. To disagree with the experts was, and is, to be a 'denier', and should lead to the perpetrator's expulsion from public life and even private career.

Even giving a platform to a critical voice is beyond the pale. For example, when the former chancellor of the exchequer and climate-change sceptic, Nigel Lawson, appeared on Radio 4's *Today* programme back in 2017, it was Brian Cox who tweeted: 'Irresponsible and highly misleading to give the impression that there is a meaningful debate about the science.' Cox certainly seemed to believe that there is a thing called The Science three years ago.

We need to get beyond a simple black-and-white view of science and expertise. The question is not whether we should believe experts, but how we understand expertise. Each and every claim needs to be treated with scepticism (not cynicism) and we need to be clear about the limits of each claim.

To go back to Blunkett's points, it really does seem that the over-70s are at greater risk from Covid-19 than younger people. That doesn't mean it necessarily makes sense to keep them under house arrest and separated from their families indefinitely. That's a judgement that involves questions of physical and mental health, autonomy, pleasure, and much more.

Carbon dioxide may be heating our planet. But the wilder claims about an overheating planet and eco-geddon need to be understood in the context of, for example, the assumptions made by computer models – some of which are actually very overheated themselves. Moreover, even if we are heading for a much warmer world, abandoning fossil fuels for a 'Net Zero' future seems to many people (including me) very likely to cause much more harm than global warming. These are matters for public debate. They should not be closed down because of The Science.

In the midst of a health crisis, hopefully we are now developing a proper and very healthy scepticism towards experts.

30 APRIL 2020

NATURE IS A BASTARD

PATRICK WEST

In Western culture, 'nature' and that which is 'natural' is usually evoked as something benign, pure, innocent and uncontaminated. 'Nature' relates to the way things should be – the natural order of things. This association is manifest most clearly in television adverts, where 'natural' is used to convey the message that a product is harmless and harmonious. It has sprung forth unmolested from Mother Earth. It's an implicit opposite to 'manmade', that which is potentially perilous because its inherent purity has been violated by *Homo sapiens*.

At a deep level, this myth of natural goodness has its origins in Christianity and the notion that mankind is a fallen creature, who once inhabited the untainted Garden of Eden before his innate immorality got the better of him. It's a myth that has been repeated and reinforced over the centuries, by Jean-Jacques Rousseau in the 18th century, who lauded man in the childlike 'state of nature'. It gained traction soon after in the Romantic reaction to the Industrial Revolution, as epitomised by William Blake's lament about those 'dark Satanic mills'. In more recent decades, the supposedly benevolent qualities of the 'natural' and 'organic' have been espoused by the environmentalist movement, in response to the perceived deleterious effect man has had on the planet, whether it be pollution, industrialised farming, nuclear disaster or climate change.

All the same, it has always been a myth. And a staggeringly ludicrous, even risible myth at that. The reality of nature is this: disease, pain, parasitism, predation, cancer, infant mortality, brain tumours, faeces, wisdom teeth, eczema, infection, plagues, tempests, earthquakes, madness, ageing, decrepitude, death – and deadly viruses. All these things are natural.

Nature in a benign light is something beautiful to behold, if we consider the lilies in the field, or raindrops on roses and whiskers on kittens. But nature's malign aspect is a thing of awe and terror: cold, cunning, savage and utterly indifferent. Foul and visceral, ferocious and scheming — 'all swoll'n and ulcerous, pitiful to the eye', as Shakespeare put it.

At the moment, many people are beginning to talk of the coronavirus from an imagined future point of view — namely, what we will have remembered from this dreadful affair in, say, six months. It is hoped that we will have remembered the sense of community, how our neighbours came to our aid, how we kept in touch with relatives via Zoom, how for weeks we diligently kept ourselves indoors and metres apart for the greater good.

I do hope we remember all this. I do indeed hope all survivors will be grateful for being alive and live every day like a cancer survivor does: in joy and gratitude. But I also hope we take away a more sober, rational lesson. I hope that we will remember the death, fear, paranoia and utter boredom inflicted upon the entire world in the spring of 2020 at the hands not of nasty mankind — which usually gets the blame for these things — but by nature, by a natural virus.

Nature is not our friend. Nature is a bastard: red in tooth and claw. Nature is mankind's eternal enemy. Our lot is a perpetual war against it. We may be of nature, but, unique to all species on this planet, we are not slaves to its lethal diktats. We transcend our origins. This is why we have always had medicines and doctors, and in more recent centuries, hospitals to treat the poorly, and scientists to invent cures and vaccines to address nature's deadly defects. Without all of this, life would be very nasty, brutish and short indeed.

I MAY 2020

I DID NOT KILL GEORGE FLOYD

BRENDAN O'NEILL

There's a new sin. Forget gluttony. Forget sloth. The great moral error today is whiteness. To be white is to be fallen. Whiteness has become a kind of original sin, an inherited moral defect one must atone for throughout one's life. In the wake of the brutal execution of George Floyd by police in Minneapolis, this almost religious treatment of whiteness as an existential flaw has gone mainstream.

Listen to the Archbishop of Canterbury. He called on 'white Christians' to 'repent of our own prejudices'. Repent, ye sinners! Or if you prefer your leaders to be secular, how about the high priestess of middle-class decency, Nigella Lawson, who instructs her fellow white people to 'acknowledge [that] systematic racism exists' and that we are 'complicit in it'. That brutal killing in Minneapolis – it's your doing, white people.

Or read *Time*, the most mainstream magazine in existence. 'White people', says one of its contributors, 'have inherited this house of white supremacy, built by their forebears and willed to them'. *Inherited*. The sins of the father *shall* be visited upon the son. The *Time* writer says white racism is a spectrum, stretching from those white people who tell a black woman 'how pretty our hair looks when we wear it straight' to 'the more extreme end of the spectrum ... cops literally suffocating black people like George Floyd as they beg for their lives'.

To compare a compliment about a woman's hair to the merciless killing of Floyd is deeply disturbing. It sanitises the crime committed against Floyd and debases his suffering by putting it on a par with a mere uninvited compliment. It also confirms how thoroughly whiteness has been pathologised in mainstream ideology. What was once said about black men – that it is problematic when they compliment women of another race and that their racial make-up drives them towards murderous behaviour – is now said about white men. Perhaps someone can explain how replacing one form of racial fatalism with another is progressive.

Whiteness-as-sin is everywhere. 'White America, if you want to know who's responsible for racism, look in the mirror', cries the *Chicago Tribune*. 'White people, you are the problem', it continues, in case you didn't get its message that this sinful race, these fallen people, are the scourge of our time.

'I'm talking about white people', said James Corden in his monologue on *The Late Late Show* in the wake of Floyd's death. 'This is our problem to solve', he said of the murder of Floyd and the problem of racism. White people, all of you, you did this. This is how mainstream the pathologisation of whiteness has become: it is now beamed into suburban living rooms across the US by famously inoffensive TV hosts. A white man telling white people about the sins of white complicity – this is, at the very least, an extremely odd state of affairs.

Let's be clear about what is happening here: this is an effort to establish racial collective guilt for the murderous suffocation of George Floyd. There are two problems with this approach. The first is that collective guilt on the basis of racial origin is always a wicked ideology to pursue. Whether it's Jews being held collectively guilty of the alleged excesses of 'rich Jews' or blacks being collectively punished for the offences of individual black people, such racial extrapolation always leads to prejudice and suffering. There is a twisted irony in the fact that so many commentators and activists who pose as anti-racist are promoting the ideology of collective racial guilt in response to the killing of George Floyd.

The second problem with this sweeping anti-white reaction to Floyd's death, and with the pathologisation of whiteness more broadly, is that it acts as a distraction from the real problems facing the United States and other societies. Collectivising the crime committed by four police officers in Minneapolis turns attention away from the specificity of police brutality and of structural disarray in modern America, in favour of pursuing a blanket suspicion of all whites. The problem is dissipated, then obscured. We are implicitly discouraged from seriously analysing specific residual political problems in the United States in favour of joining in the thrill-inducing project of bashing all whites.

It is important to understand where this distracting moral project comes from. It is an outlook of the privileged elites, very often white elites. It comes from academia, from the media class, from the younger members of the political establishment. For years now, these privileged elites have promoted hostility to whiteness.

They have projected the sins of the past on to whites living today, claiming that white people are the beneficiaries of slavery and colonialism. They have pushed the ideology of 'white complicity' (that is, all whites bear responsibility for racial crimes) and 'white fragility' (that is, any white who pushes back against this idea of collective racial guilt is showing his moral weakness). They have encouraged the checking of one's white privilege, which is really a modern form of penance.

Anyone who thought the cranky woke idea of privilege-checking was confined to PC campuses will have had a rude awakening over the past few days. We've had the Archbishop of Canterbury promoting a Christian version of white self-correction. And anyone who has seen the incredibly creepy videos showing groups of white people begging black people for forgiveness for the historic crimes of racism, or chanting in a massive crowd about how they will do better in future, will know that privilege-checking has become the new religion. Original sin, repentance, public self-flagellation – it has it all.

Anti-whiteness comes from the top. It is most pronounced among privileged whites. It has nothing in common with the noble struggles for racial equality in the past. Rather, it expresses the nihilism and fatalism of the contemporary liberal elites and intellectual classes. It is self-loathing disguised as radicalism. It is not the friend, by any stretch of the imagination, of black people or white people. On the contrary, it condemns both to an interminable status quo in which the former must perform the role of perennial victim and the latter must engage in penitence, publicly and noisily, forever. Elite fatalism sees no way out of inequality or injustice, precisely because it has reimagined these things as 'traits', as the *Chicago Tribune* puts it, of racial behaviour. All it can envisage is a technocratic system of racial management in which black victims are encouraged to speak and weep and whites are encouraged to listen and repent. Like a forever truth and reconciliation commission.

It is striking that where past black campaigners for racial equality spoke in terms of visions, dreams and better futures in which things would be different, today's self-styled correctors of white privilege can only obsess over the past. History is their stomping ground. Slavery and colonialism are their obsessions. A writer for *Slate* says these things are America's 'original sin' and George Floyd's murder shows that they infect us still. This sums up the fatalism of the new racial guardians. In describing racism as America's 'original sin', they utterly demean the agency of the black people, and white people, who fought for rights and equality over the centuries and who tangibly changed America for the better. Worse, they lock America into racial permanence, into round after round of racial accusation and racial repentance, into a never-ending self-whipping for the inherited sins of the past. It is an entirely dispiriting ideology that offers nothing whatsoever to blacks and whites fighting for freer, better futures.

This is why corporate America and the new political elites have no problem at all with the woke ideology of pathologised whiteness. In fact they embrace it. In recent days some of the most powerful corporations in the US have commented on the problem of 'white supremacy'. Leaders and officials in Minneapolis and elsewhere initially refused to condemn rioting on the basis that, as white people, it wasn't their place to do so. The academia-born new racialism can be easily internalised by the capitalist and political elites because it poses no threat whatsoever to their influence over society. On the contrary, in dissipating the problems of racism and social inequality, in personalising these things and reducing them to 'traits' that exist across the whole of society, the woke ideology takes the heat off the powers-that-be and even creates a space for them to perform their penitence and advertise their awareness and in the process become part of the 'saved' people. It empowers them.

This is the great tragedy in the US right now. People are on the streets marching and arguing for some kind of change, but the dominant political ideology and language of our time utterly fails to meet their expectations or even to allow that meaningful change is possible. In accepting today's ruling-class ideology – the ideology of wokeness and of forever racialism – the leaders of these protests have defeated themselves already. They have embraced an ideology that makes solidarity virtually impossible, by constantly flagging the differential 'traits' between blacks and whites, and which elevates backward-looking historic repentance over moving towards a better, wealthier future.

George Floyd's death has exposed how dominant, destructive and futile the woke worldview has become. Rejecting the new racialism, spurning the woke creed, turning one's back on elite fatalism that today comes in the garb of caring about black people – these are the preconditions for proper solidarity and real change.

3 JUNE 2020

RIP NEW YORK TIMES

SEAN COLLINS

The *New York Times* is a legendary American cultural institution. Founded in 1851, its nickname is 'the Gray Lady', bestowed for its reputation as a sober and impartial 'paper of record'. The breadth and openness of the *Times'* traditional liberal vision is summed up by its slogan, 'All the news that's fit to print', with the emphasis on 'all'.

But the leaders of today's *Times* have decided to throw some 170 years of liberalism in the dustbin of history. Bowing to a threatened 'virtual walkout' from its younger and woker staff, the *Times* has sacked its opinion editor, James Bennet. What so offended these employees? An op-ed from a sitting senator that called for the military to back up the National Guard to control rioting in certain cities in the wake of the killing of George Floyd. This view had majority support among Americans at the time of publication, and was an issue debated in other media. But it was deemed too 'dangerous' for the pages of the *New York Times* by its sensitive staff.

The extraordinary campaign to denounce the opinion piece, written by Republican senator Tom Cotton, began when *Times* employees began tweeting the same sentence *en masse*: 'Running this puts Black @nytimes staff in danger.' The News Guild (a union) called it 'a clear threat to the health and safety of the journalists we represent'. To old-time journalists, the idea that an op-ed could be physically threatening might seem odd. But those who know woke politics would recognise the formulation: words can cause violence. At the same time, the *Times'* staff who claim to fear for their own safety due to a senator's words are the same ones who have declared violent rioting to be mere 'protests' and the exercise of free speech.

Initially, the powers-that-be at the *Times* defended the publication of Cotton's piece, providing a standard liberal rationale. Bennet tweeted: 'Times Opinion owes it to our readers to show them counter-arguments, particularly those made by people in a position to set policy. We understand that many readers find Senator Cotton's argument painful, even dangerous. We believe that is one reason it requires public scrutiny and debate.' The publisher, AG Sulzberger, said: 'I believe in the principle of openness to a range of opinions, even those we may disagree with, and this piece was published in that spirit.'

These are admirable statements to those of a liberal persuasion. But after an internal staff meeting, Sulzberger abandoned any liberal principles he may have had and caved in to the woke mob. The *Times* apologised for publishing the op-ed, saying 'the essay fell short of our standards', and blamed a 'rushed and flawed' editorial process. An 'editors' note' was attached to the offending piece, claiming that Cotton made assertions that were uncorroborated, and used a tone that was 'needlessly harsh'. But these were simply excuses to justify an embarrassing climbdown. Then, on Sunday, Sulzberger decided Bennet had to go. The woke coup was complete.

Watching this play out, it was hard to avoid hearing echoes of Evergreen State College and other uprisings of offended woke students. In both cases, adults, seemingly in charge, are humiliated in meetings reminiscent of Maoist struggle sessions. Having mouthed so many platitudes about diversity and psychological wellbeing themselves, these supposed authority figures find themselves defenceless when called on it by their more morally strident youth charges. And when the younger generation present a form of emotional blackmail – 'do what I say or you will be blamed for harming me, a person of colour' – the older generation is too scared to stand up for liberal values, and acquiesces to the mob.

But we have to pinch ourselves and remember – this is not Evergreen State College, this is the *New York Times*. It's a bigger deal than a few campus radicals creating a fuss. The capture of such an august institution by the intolerant and illiberal woke set is a major milestone in the ongoing decline of liberalism.

This change, it should be noted, has not come suddenly to the *Times*. An analysis, conducted by Zach Goldberg, found a very sharp rise in the *Times*' use of phrases like 'social justice' and other woke terminology starting around 2014. More recently, it abandoned any pretence of objectivity and led the charge in accusing Trump of collusion with Russia. In 2019, the *Times* launched its '1619 Project', which argues that the US is founded on the principle of slavery and can never escape its legacy. Despite being ridiculed by leading historians for promoting multiple falsehoods, the *Times* has led a campaign to push '1619' into schools, consolidating its shift from reporting to advocacy.

But, however long in development, the woke mutiny at the *Times* is a watershed moment for US society and culture generally. It seems that the protests over George Floyd's death, and the rise of Black Lives Matter, are becoming a catalyst for a movement to purge old-think in the media. The top editor at the *Philadelphia Inquirer* was also forced to resign recently, after publishing a piece with the headline 'Buildings Matter, Too' (a piece that highlighted the negative consequences of the rioting for the black community). Stan Wischnowski was with the newspaper for 20 years, won Pulitzer prizes and increased the hiring of minority staff. But no matter, the article was too offensive – he had to go. Who, of the older generation of editors, is next?

Meanwhile, the *Times* looks headed towards taking a harder line against free thinking. In her first note to staff, Katie Kingsbury, the new acting head of opinion, said: 'Any piece of Opinion journalism – including headlines or social posts or photos or you name it – that gives you the slightest pause, please call or text me immediately.' That's right, all *Times* employees are now empowered to report on those who deviate from the new moral mission.

What's even worse is the corruption of the news side of the business. Although I prefer a diversity of views, I'm fine if the opinion section of a newspaper ultimately expresses a political bias. But, as the latest purges at the *Times* now confirm, its news reporters are driven by a woke agenda, too – and that means it is hard to trust even the most basic news stories. Indeed, it was revealing that so many from the *Times* newsroom were leading the charge against their colleagues in the opinion department. Do not expect news stories that raise questions about Black Lives Matter.

The *Times* is keeping its slogan, 'All the news that's fit to print'. But going forward, expect to see the paper emphasise the word 'fit', rather than the word 'all'. Its staff will ensure that any thought that doesn't 'fit' with the woke agenda will be expunged from its pages.

Over the decades, the *New York Times* didn't always live up to its liberal ideals, but at least it had them. The paper, on the whole, had a positive impact on promoting a liberal outlook in American life. But no more. RIP.

9 JUNE 2020

WE NEED TO TALK ABOUT BLACK LIVES MATTER

ANDREW DOYLE

At times of heightened emotion, discussion is always difficult.
It is impossible to see the footage of George Floyd's murder at the
hands of a Minneapolis police officer without feeling anger at this
utter disregard for human life. The police are uniquely licensed
to use force against citizens in the interests of upholding law and
order, and so it is essential that we are vigilant against abuses of
this power. Any instances of police brutality or racism need to be
opposed with vigour, and the peaceful protesters who have done
so deserve our support.

Such campaigns are inevitably undermined when they are
hijacked by ideological groups with other agendas, or those who
resort to violence. The ensuing confusion explains why in recent
days we have seen major media outlets and politicians defending
and even encouraging violent action. Some who have condemned
looting, arson and physical attacks have even been accused of
supporting white supremacy, a vile and disingenuous charge that
is almost certainly intended to quash dissent. This has largely come
about because activists, many of them white and middle class,
have taken the opportunity to exploit a worthy cause. The essential
work of standing up against police brutality, as evinced by the
unforgivable treatment of Floyd, is being obscured by a culture
war that is freewheeling out of control.

Those of us who have urged vigilance when it comes to the rise
of identity politics and the cult of 'social justice' have now been
fully vindicated. For years we have warned about the ways in which
the culture war had the potential to infect all public and political
discourse. But we were dismissed as railing against niche politics

confined to campus common rooms and the dark recesses of the internet. Now the culture war has exploded on to the streets of the US and UK. If that sounds like a fancy way to say 'I told you so', then so be it.

If we are to have any chance of preserving the liberal values upon which our society depends, we need to find a way to navigate the binary thinking that comes with ideologically driven movements. The first step is to acknowledge common ground. In all my life I have never met a single person who would not agree with the proposition that 'black lives matter', so that seems like a good place to start. It's been many years since racism has been in any way tolerated by polite society, one of the undeniably positive outcomes of the political-correctness campaigns of the 1980s and 1990s. A further point on which we can surely all agree is that racism exists and should be resisted wherever it occurs. This may seem obvious, but since any opposition to the cult of social justice is automatically taken as a denial of the fact of racism, it is worth making the point explicitly.

Those who would deny the existence of racism, or do not agree that black lives matter, or do not accept that racism is an evil that must always be confronted, are already beyond the scope of rational adult conversation. The vast majority of the population believe in our shared values of equality and fairness, although many social-justice activists prefer to ignore this reality in favour of a fantasy Britain awash with fascists. We saw this in the way that Brexit voters were consistently smeared as xenophobic, even though such a label could only possibly apply to a tiny minority. We saw this in the myth that those who voted Leave were nostalgic for a colonial past, a virtually non-existent mindset that was assumed to be commonplace on the basis of no evidence at all. These kinds of prejudices, largely levelled against working-class people by bourgeois commentators, in turn generated the kind of resentment that almost certainly tipped the scales in favour of Brexit and ultimately led to the collapse of Labour's 'Red Wall'. These outcomes were in themselves taken as proof of Britain's inherent racism, and so we find ourselves caught in this perpetual square dance of straw men.

All of which has been a boon for the intersectional, identity-based social-justice movement, which is sustained on a view of society that bears little resemblance to reality. The latest protests have been infiltrated, and often stoked, by the presence of various groups who unite under the banner of 'Antifa'. Like 'Black Lives Matter', these groups rely on the good nature of a public that is likely to interpret their name literally. After all, only a fascist would complain about anti-fascism. Even Mara Liasson, national political correspondent for NPR, fell for this basic rhetorical trick when she described the Normandy landing of more than 150,000 Allied troops as the 'biggest Antifa rally in history'. Activist singer Billy Bragg posted an image of Winston Churchill captioned simply with 'ANTIFA'. That protesters this week defaced the statue of Churchill in Parliament Square and branded him a 'racist' shows the incoherence of much of what is going on.

To return to our common ground: not only is fascism vanishingly rare in the UK, but you would also be hard pushed to find anyone who isn't wholeheartedly opposed to fascism. We are all anti-fascist, which makes Antifa's claim to be resisting a popular tyrannous force seem about 80 years out of date. The difference is that most of us understand that pepper-spraying a Trump supporter, or striking a UKIP voter over the head with a bike lock, doesn't put us in the same bracket as those who fought actual fascists at Cable Street in 1936.

Our failure to instil critical thinking in our education system has led to many of the problems we face in today's society. To make the case for measured and reasonable discussion of these sensitive issues is to open oneself up to entirely unfounded charges of racism. In such circumstances, most people would rather acquiesce for the sake of an easy life. We have even seen those who have raised questions about the wisdom of permitting mobs to destroy public landmarks being accused of endorsing the slave trade. 'How you feel about that statue is how you feel about slavery', tweeted LBC presenter James O'Brien, referring to the statue of slave trader Edward Colston that was toppled by protesters in Bristol. But the chances of finding anyone in the UK who would defend slavery are infinitesimal, and it is surely inconceivable that anyone making these allegations sincerely believes otherwise.

But the media and political classes are not interested in serious debate about the aims of the protesters. They would rather uncritically declare their fealty for fear of being mischaracterised. Corporations are likewise competing with each other to emphasise their solidarity. PG Tips and Yorkshire Tea have been quick to rebuke customers via Twitter for any signs of non-conformity, as though their values extend any further than the mass distribution of tea for financial gain. Politicians are 'taking the knee' for photo opportunities, and London mayor Sadiq Khan is consulting with 'diversity experts' to determine which historical landmarks ought to be removed. A campaign to #ShutDownAcademia and #ShutDownSTEM is gaining momentum, with academics calling for more inclusive 'new ways of knowing' and asserting that higher education, like all major cultural institutions, is 'systemically racist'.

Meanwhile, major television streaming services are frantically deleting content that might cause offence. *Little Britain* has been removed from BBC iPlayer for its comedic 'blackface'. Netflix has followed suit — in addition to *Little Britain*, the service has taken down *The Mighty Boosh* and *The League Of Gentlemen*. And *Gone With The Wind* has lived up to its name, now excised from HBO Max with the possibility that it will return at a later date with a 'discussion of its historical context'. Such decisions are almost certainly well intentioned, but they are based on the patronising belief that viewers are incapable of understanding how ethical standards change over time.

More common ground is available here should we wish to seize it. The Antebellum South that we see depicted in *Gone With The Wind* was indubitably racist. History is replete with examples of systemic racism that would never be condoned today, so we should always take seriously any possibility that systemic racism still lurks in our society. But when activists make the claim that UK universities in 2020 are hotbeds of white supremacy, we are right to ask for clear and irrefutable proof. These are among the most tolerant places to live and work, and so in this case the proposition of systemic racism needs to be discussed and investigated, not assumed. For one thing, the data make it clear that racist incidents on UK campuses are rare. That is not to say that the research might not be flawed, but unless we can have a sensible discussion, few will be persuaded to change their minds.

We are fortunate to live in a country in which it is illegal to discriminate on the basis of race. Even the suggestion that anyone has done so is enough to ruin his or her livelihood and reputation. As liberals, we should be tackling instances of racism as and when they occur, not making faith-based claims of nebulous 'power structures' and ascribing collective guilt on the basis of skin colour. In the late 1960s, Hannah Arendt criticised the 'rather fashionable' tendency among white liberals to accept collective guilt, which she described as 'the best possible safeguard against the discovery of culprits'. In this, she was articulating something that we all instinctively know. 'Where all are guilty, no one is', she wrote. 'The real rift between black and white is not healed by being translated into an even less reconcilable conflict between collective innocence and collective guilt.' Yet this is now precisely the kind of conflict that is being fostered. Any claim of systemic racism should be the beginning of a conversation, not the end.

Similarly, we must feel able to discuss movements such as Black Lives Matter critically, and not simply assume that its objectives are straightforwardly encapsulated by its name. How many people know, for instance, that part of the Black Lives Matter manifesto is a commitment to 'dismantle cisgender privilege' and 'disrupt the Western-prescribed nuclear family structure requirement by supporting each other as extended families and "villages" that collectively care for one another'? The movement, in other words, is not solely about standing up to racism, a goal that anyone with an intact moral compass would share. Look carefully at the messages of the graffiti and the placards on many of these protests. Yes, we all agree that black lives matter, but can we really say the same for 'All Cops Are Bastards' or 'Fuck Madeleine McCann'?

That we have reached the point at which the majority of people are genuinely afraid of having difficult conversations is a tragedy for everyone. We are right to be concerned when mobs are able to decide which historical monuments should be destroyed through force of intimidation. We are right to object to groundless accusations of racism as a means to stifle discussion. We are right to be appalled when people are hounded out of their jobs for wrongthink. We are right to be nervous about race-based collective guilt. We are right to challenge the wisdom of removing offensive content from entertainment services or libraries. We are right to promote compassion and empathy in the face of those who would sooner dehumanise and bully anyone who questions their ideological worldview. We are right to decry violence when so many are seemingly oblivious to the sanctity of human life. We are right to be worried when racial division is being sown in the name of anti-racism. We are right to be alert to the signs of a creeping form of authoritarianism that conceals itself beneath a veneer of social justice. Above all, we are right to risk standing up for the values of a liberal democracy in the maelstrom of a seemingly endless culture war.

12 JUNE 2020

SILENCE IS NOT VIOLENCE

MICK HUME

The slogan 'Silence is Violence', which has appeared in Black Lives Matter protests in the US, the UK and around the world, is a powerful and emotive message. It is also, however, a danger to freedom of speech – the same freedom that has been central to struggles for liberty and against oppression.

For years I have written about the powerful culture of 'You Can't Say That' in Western societies. But the war on any speech deemed offensive or hateful has recently become far more intense.

Now, in addition to 'You Can't Say That', we are faced with a new order: 'You Must Say This.' The slogan 'Silence is Violence' does not only mean that you must speak out, but that you must also follow the correct script. You are free to say exactly what everybody else is saying, and say it loud.

Free speech must always involve the right to offend, to speak what you believe to be true regardless of what others think. The flipside of free speech is that you must have the right to be silent when you choose – particularly when somebody is trying to compel you to speak as instructed. What is called 'compelled speech' has long been opposed by civil-liberties campaigners, notably in the US. Now it is apparently embraced by woke activists.

How did we get here? It began with the increasingly influential but misplaced idea that words are at least as bad as physical violence and should be policed as strictly. In response, it has been important to remind ourselves that free speech is simply speech; no matter how harsh or forceful words might be, they are not bullets or knives. And that speech must be free for all or for none at all.

These days things have moved on. We are now told not only that speech is violence, but also that silence is violence. The message is that if you fail to toe the line in public and don't repeat the mantras of the Black Lives Matter movement, then you must be guilty of racism, or at least be complicit in the racist system. Young people have come under tremendous pressure to publish the approved messages and images on social media, something that has disturbed even some of those sympathetic to BLM. Even woke celebrities have come under fire for failing to use exactly the right words in their posts, as if they were expected to repeat a religious text.

(We might note in passing that, at the same time as speech is condemned as violence and silence is said to be violence, sometimes the actual violence of protesters is apparently not seen as violence, so long as you approve of what they're protesting for.)

There currently seems to be considerable interest in the history of oppression. One aspect worthy of further enquiry might be the history of 'compelled speech', of being forced to say what you are told rather than what you think. Compelled speech has a long association with intolerant and totalitarian regimes, as captured in the compulsory 'Two Minutes Hate' for party members to scream at Big Brother's enemies in George Orwell's *Nineteen Eighty-Four*.

Even in democratic states, there is a history of seeking to impose conformism in thought and speech, both through informal measures and the law. In America, the First Amendment to the US Constitution enshrines the right to freedom of speech. Campaigners against compelled speech have previously succeeded in getting the Supreme Court to recognise that the First Amendment also upholds the freedom not to speak, by refusing to repeat government propaganda or to toe the line of any political group.

In the past, compelled speech was commonly associated with authoritarians and traditionalists. Now it is the woke activists who want to police speech through their 'Silence is Violence' campaign. People are faced with the prospect of being shunned and effectively 'cancelled' unless they conform and repeat the right messages in public. There is no choice about what you say or think, no questions tolerated. In a sign of changed times, the American Civil Liberties Union has all but abandoned its campaigns for free speech for all and against compelled speech.

In the face of this outburst of radical intolerance, it is surely important to insist that it is possible to be entirely opposed to racism and at the same time to be absolutely in favour of free speech – including freedom from compelled speech.

More than that, fighting for free speech has been key to every struggle for liberation and equality. As the former slave and campaigner against slavery in America, Frederick Douglass, put it in 1860, 'Liberty is meaningless where the right to utter one's thoughts and opinions has ceased to exist. That, of all rights, is the dread of tyrants. It is the right which they first of all strike down. They know its power ... Slavery cannot tolerate free speech.'

Those who want to stand for liberty, equality and justice, on the other hand, should surely tolerate free speech: the liberty 'to utter one's thoughts and opinions', or to say nothing at all, rather than repeating what you are instructed to think and say – no matter who is giving the orders.

16 JUNE 2020

HOW TRANS TOOK OVER

JOANNA WILLIAMS

Amid the recent clamour to denounce JK Rowling for her sacrilegious utterance of the word 'woman' comes some good news. A slipped-out UK government announcement has revealed – at long last – some badly needed pushback against the demands of transgender activists. The government is expected to drop plans to allow transgender people to change their birth certificates without a medical diagnosis, and to put in place new protections to safeguard female-only spaces such as refuges and prisons.

This is not before time. The drawn-out conflict between defenders of sex-based rights and believers in gender self-identification has benefitted no one. And, let's not forget, this was a conflict largely prompted by a Conservative government. It was back in 2018, on Theresa May's watch, that the consultation to the Gender Recognition Act (2004) was launched, paving the way for gender self-identification and calling into question once taken-for-granted assumptions about biology, sex and what it means to be a woman.

But to understand how institutions such as the police, prisons, schools and medical services became so transfixed by the ideology of transgenderism that they were prepared to jettison the safe-guarding of children and turn back the clock on women's hard-won rights, we have to look beyond government announcements and consultations. We need to ask how, in little more than two decades, 'transgender' morphed from a term representing individuals, and little used outside of specialist communities, to one signifying a powerful political ideology driving significant social change.

We need to ask how children – often girls with autism or suffering with mental-health problems – could so easily find themselves heading down a path leading to surgery. We need to ask why teenage girls were expected to get changed for PE or try on clothes in shops alongside boys. We need to ask why incarcerated women could be sexually assaulted by male inmates and why women escaping domestic violence could end up in a shelter with men. Why were so many people in positions of power within the realms of media, education, academia, police, social work, medicine, law and government prepared to coalesce behind the demands of a tiny group of transgender activists?

In part, this political and policy success was down to strategies consciously adopted by key figures within the transgender movement. Deliberate efforts were made to align campaigns for transgender rights with pre-existing gay-rights groups – adding the 'T' to the LGB movement. Significantly, this allowed access to already established networks and funding at a time when, with the legalisation of same-sex marriage, gay rights had largely been achieved. When it came to advocating for changes to the Gender Recognition Act, transgender activists were in a position to set out the key issue – self-identification – before feminist groups were fully aware of what was at stake. Indeed, transgender activists deliberately targeted certain women's groups to gain acceptance for their view that gender was entirely based in the brain.

One masterstroke by transgender activists was the refusal to debate. Any attempt at rational discussion, any recognition that there may be competing rights at stake, was met by accusations of calling into question the right of transgender people to exist. Another, even more shameful ploy was hiding an adult agenda behind concern for the plight of children. For activists in the transgender movement, the existence and increasing visibility of transgender children provided evidence for their claims that transgender people are 'born that way' and that identifying with a different gender to your anatomical sex is an intrinsic part of a person's psyche. The beatification of transgender children as vulnerable, but also brave and politically progressive, rubbed off on their defenders. This, in turn, provided transgender adults with a layer of protection from criticism and questioning and legitimised demands being made of educators, health professionals and policymakers.

But the actions taken by a small number of transgender activists, no matter how shrewd or calculating, are not sufficient to explain the widespread reshaping of social institutions and cultural conventions that has taken place in recent years. None of this could have happened without a readiness from people outside of the transgender community and in positions of authority not only to accept having their language and policies policed, but also to go further – to play a role in affirming the gender ideology promoted by campaigners and, in the process, enforcing speech and behaviour codes.

The reasons for this acquiescence lie in our broader political climate, in particular the rise of identity politics and the emergence of a culture of victimhood. Transgender people are exploited as the living embodiment of a challenge to a supposedly outdated, binary, heteronormative order. Advocating on behalf of the 'transgender community' allows others to be associated with this identity-driven challenge to convention. It provides institutions with a sense of purpose and legitimacy for action that comes with the readymade moral authority of protecting the oppressed.

The government's decision to back down on proposed changes to the Gender Recognition Act will have come as a relief to many. But the grip transgender ideology has on our culture and institutions remains. For instance, a school in West Sussex recently dropped plans to name one of its houses after JK Rowling following her tweets in defence of women. This is a shameful message to send to children. Rowling should be a role model for her life story, her achievements and her strength of character in standing up to social-media bullies.

National policy change is a small step in the right direction. But if we really want to challenge the corrosive impact of the transgender ideology, we need to win a bigger social, cultural and political argument. We need to understand how transgenderism was able to gain such a tight grip on our institutions so that we do not end up in this position again.

19 JUNE 2020

WOKE, INC.

FRASER MYERS

It can't have escaped people's notice that the Black Lives Matter protests that erupted in the wake of the brutal killing of George Floyd have had the overwhelming backing of the capitalist elites.

Social media were awash with black squares as every brand under the sun took part in #BlackoutTuesday in favour of the protests. Apple – the world's wealthiest tech company – replaced all of the radio stations on its music app with a single stream of songs by black artists, including NWA's 'Fuck Tha Police'. Lego – the world's largest toy company – pulled advertising for its police-related toys. Ben & Jerry's ice-cream – owned by Unilever, one of the world's largest consumer-goods producers – made a solemn promise to 'dismantle white supremacy'. The very few companies that didn't take part were loudly denounced and heads were made to roll.

Fox News was widely criticised for producing a tasteless graphic that highlighted the stock-market gains in the immediate aftermath of George Floyd's murder. It also compared them with the gains made following similar racist atrocities in the US. It showed that the S&P rose by 3.4 per cent following Floyd's killing. This was compared with a rise of just 2.9 per cent following Martin Luther King's assassination (which sparked the riots of 1968), and 1.2 per cent after both the acquittal of the police officers who brutalised Rodney King (leading to the LA riots of 1992) and the police killing of Michael Brown (which sparked the Ferguson uprising of 2014).

The Fox graphic said the quiet part out loud – that the brutal execution of an innocent black man would be a good opportunity for business. Why? Because it would offer every brand the opportunity to restate its commitment to the vaguely defined values of diversity and inclusion and to present itself as a force for progress in a cruel, heartless and reactionary world. This is surely what Jamie Dimon, the CEO of JPMorgan Chase (America's largest bank), was communicating when he 'took the knee' in front of a giant open bank vault.

On the whole, wokeness is good for business. According to an Edelman survey of 35 countries, 64 per cent of customers say they would reward firms for taking a stand on social issues. This isn't a foolproof strategy. Gillette showed it was possible to 'go woke and go broke' when it insulted its male consumer base by deriding 'toxic masculinity' in one of its adverts. But in general, the risks are low and 'taking a stand' is inexpensive, while the rewards are potentially high. When Nike launched an advertising campaign with NFL player Colin Kaepernick – who had been sacked for taking the knee – its sales were boosted by billions.

Some have questioned whether companies are as committed to social-justice causes as they claim. The BBC, for instance, notes that many of the firms that have praised Black Lives Matter have very few black people in leadership positions. Others have noted that the employment practices of those who supply the likes of Nike and Apple in the developing world are not all that unlike slavery. But overwhelmingly, it seems that woke gestures are enough to burnish a brand's reputation.

Consider Dow Chemical, a company that made napalm for the US military during the Vietnam War. It is also considered to be liable for the world's worst industrial disaster – the Bhopal gas tragedy, which killed at least 3,000 people. In 2019, *Bloomberg Businessweek* devoted a feature to how 'Dow Chemical got woke'. The standfirst featured the following astonishing sentence, which seemed to imply that the second half cancelled out the first: 'The big conservative chemical company with a legacy of making napalm during the Vietnam War has a gay CEO.' Wokeness absolves all sins, it seems.

It is easy to portray these moves as mere cynicism or 'woke-washing'. But the embrace of these values by the corporate world is very real. Capitalism has struggled to justify its existence for decades, especially since the dawn of the Long Depression from the 1970s onwards. It has stagnated and struggled to provide Westerners with the growing abundance we once expected, though it has managed to coast in the knowledge that there is no serious alternative. Wokeness offers the capitalist class a new sense of mission and moral purpose. There is a similar dynamic at play with 'sustainability' and green capitalism.

And it's not just brands that are benefitting. A whole diversity-and-inclusion industry has emerged. According to Iris Bohnet, in an interview with McKinsey consultants, US companies spend an estimated $8 billion annually on diversity training alone. Bohnet could not find any evidence that this has led to increased diversity. Yet corporate enthusiasm for diversity remains undiminished. It is a mission without end.

Private consultancy on race and diversity can be a good money-spinner, too. The book *White Fragility* recently rocketed back to the top of the *New York Times* bestseller list. Its (white) author, Robin DiAngelo, is a corporate consultant, and much of her book reads like an advert for her consultancy. It was recently discovered that one of her unlikely clients for her race-awareness training was the Trump administration.

Industries and sectors that are already diverse still insist on finding more diversity. For instance, the UK TV industry's latest Creative Diversity Network report finds that 'those who identify as female, transgender, BAME and lesbian, gay or bisexual (LGB) are all represented at levels comparable with (or above) national population estimates'. The BAME population is actually more prevalent on screen than in the country as a whole – making up 23 per cent of on-screen contributions but just 14 per cent of the population. The job of diversity seems to be largely done, but there is a lot of money available that depends on people pretending otherwise.

In the public sector, diversity and inclusion is practically a religion. Even the NHS, which everyone knows has a disproportionate number of BAME doctors and nurses, is engaged in a bizarre drive for more diversity. One in five NHS staff is BAME and a whopping 30 per cent of doctors are from an Asian background. Most normal people couldn't care less about the skin colour of the people saving their lives. Nevertheless, hospital trusts across the country are employing diversity managers, some of whom are earning around £70,000 per year from the taxpayer.

Ultimately, the question we should ask about all political movements is: who benefits? Whether Black Lives Matter and the cultural revolution unfolding in its wake has any benefit for black people on the poverty line or facing police violence is yet to be seen.

The capitalist class and the public-sector middle classes, on the other hand, have found an unparalleled opportunity for moral and spiritual renewal. They will be the guardians and facilitators of the new woke morality, and therefore its chief beneficiaries — both financially and reputationally.

19 JUNE 2020

STOP BASHING CHINA

PHIL MULLAN

The West's anti-Chinese stance has consolidated itself since the start of the Covid-19 pandemic. The Chinese government is accused of being too slow to recognise the threat of the coronavirus and of failing to alert the rest of the world. These failings are put forward as confirmation that the Chinese state represents a political and strategic threat to the US, and to the Western world more widely.

This is not to say that China's autocratic, one-party government is not deserving of criticism. From the severe restrictions imposed on freedom of speech and freedom of assembly to the persecution of the Uyghur minority in the Xinjiang region, the Chinese Communist Party (CCP) has an extensive record of authoritarian behaviour and denying its own people basic freedoms, often with brutal suppression.

But just as problems in the US are for American people to resolve, and problems within Britain are for British people to resolve, the same applies with regard to China. Repression against Chinese people, the same as the repression meted out by authoritarian regimes anywhere, will not be resolved by other governments or international bodies stepping in with economic or other weaponry. Indeed, that can make matters much worse.

Yet, unfortunately, such Western governmental confrontation is now being advocated by China-bashers. Legitimate condemnations of measures taken by the Beijing regime have turned into arguments for the Western authorities to take action against China.

Across the American political class, moves to isolate and punish China have become the accepted bipartisan stance. In Britain, senior Conservatives have attacked the Chinese government's 'aggressive economic policies', which are said to be aimed at 'dominating' the West and 'reshaping' the world in a way that 'suits autocracy'.

NATO has also joined in, with secretary-general Jens Stoltenberg claiming China's rise is 'multiplying the threats to open societies and individual freedoms, and increasing the competition over our values and our way of life'.

Today's targeting of China as a threat to the world did not come out of the blue. In fact, the ratcheting up of geopolitical pressure on China had been underway for some time. Almost a decade ago, the Obama administration made the decisive shift in identifying China as a rising threat, with its so-called pivot to Asia.

The Trans-Pacific Partnership (TPP), eventually signed in early 2016, was presented as the key economic pillar of America's Asian pivot. The TPP's geopolitical role was hard to disguise as it sought to extend ties with all the major economies in the region, but with the notable exception of China.

Trump has continued the US's move against China. The only difference is that the confrontation has taken a blunter form.

Instead of going along with contemporary China-bashing we need to work out democratic, internationalist ways to act in solidarity with the Chinese people today. The guiding principle here is that collective direct action by people to undermine the power of the CCP is going to be more helpful to democrats in China than intrusive actions taken by Western governments.

Support for the Chinese people's pursuit of popular freedom is best served, in the first instance, by people in the West standing up for their own freedoms and democratic rights. This can inspire others toward the same ends in their countries. For example, the Brexit vote in 2016, motivated by a desire to return control of laws and regulations to locally accountable bodies, was an inspiration to critics of the undemocratic EU across Europe and beyond.

What's more, China-bashing damages politics in the West. It diverts attention away from addressing the real domestic sources of problems within the Western world — political, social and economic.

It is always easy for elites to find a foreign country or a foreign force to blame for their troubles, not least because these problems often have foreign implications. Today, China serves as the primary foreign scapegoat, with Chinese economic strength identified as the cause of Western economic weakness.

But China is not responsible for Western economic weakness. The failures in the US, Britain and most other advanced industrial countries to create sufficient new businesses and sectors that can generate good jobs for the jobless are domestically rooted. They are not due to China. They are the consequence of structural economic problems that national governments have failed to address. Western elites heap blame on China to evade responsibility for their own failings.

Continuing the economic theme, not only does China-bashing dodge the domestic foundation of economic decay, it can also compound economic weakness by rolling back the economic gains of internationalisation. World society – east and west, north and south – has benefitted from the economic advantages of specialisation and economies of scale within an international division of labour.

This progress has been uneven and irregular, and not all countries have prospered to the same extent. Nevertheless, it would be regressive for governments of the advanced industrial countries to seek directly or indirectly to limit China's domestic and international economic development.

Aiming to fetter China's rise would, firstly, have adverse economic effects for the people of China. Despite being a one-party autocracy, few critics dispute that China's take-off since the late 1970s has taken about 800million people out of poverty, and raised living standards substantially across its entire population. Western attempts to isolate China could economically slow the momentum of its further expansion, and might even reverse some of the past gains in living standards for its inhabitants.

Closing off trade, investment and business relationships would also impair the economic health of the very Western countries imposing the restrictions, boycotts and sanctions. After all, even the most productive of Western businesses have come to rely on China and the rest of the East Asian region for supplies, markets and locations for production.

The potential indirect effects for prosperity and livelihoods in the rest of the world are harder to nail down, but they could also be substantial. A world economy from which China, the single most important contributor to global growth for many years, is excluded would be an economic move backwards, impacting on billions of people.

China-bashing is also potentially divisive within the West, at the expense of people of Chinese heritage who live, study and visit here. Targeting the Beijing leadership as a danger to Western interests gives sanction to a less specific sentiment directed against Chinese people in general. This would be detrimental to the Chinese, and it could spread to other East Asians, including Japanese and Koreans.

Indeed, in the early weeks of the Chinese-originated virus hitting Europe there were reports of hostility to some Chinese people, including residents of Chinese origin, in Italy, France, Canada and Britain. Although hostile incidents seemed to have been limited, this is not grounds for complacency. Fierce official China-bashing that appeals to earlier notions of a 'yellow peril' could have unpleasant and potentially violent consequences for Chinese-looking people in Western countries.

Finally, China-bashing is dangerous for global peace. In the background, a huge mismatch already exists between economic and political power in the world, with the centre of global wealth-creation shifting decisively from west to east, specifically from the US to China. Given the pandemic has had a far greater impact economically on Western industrial countries than on China, it is likely to amplify this east-west economic divergence.

The West's economic threats can easily move beyond wars of words and tariff squabbles. The co-existence of China-bashing with a more combative style of Chinese domestic and so-called Wolf Warrior foreign policy creates a vicious cycle of heightening tensions. Even if all major governments – east and west – seek to avoid military conflict, escalating confrontations can soon take a militarised form.

This danger of open conflict is aggravated by problems at home for all the main players. The Beijing regime may appear solid and secure, but so do all autocratic governments until they fall. While the lack of democratic mechanisms is explicitly built into Chinese governance, this has one drawback for the CCP politburo: it has less of a handle on where it stands in the eyes and minds of the Chinese populace. The famed 'obedience' of Chinese people may be a delusion. Uncertainty about the CCP's real grip on society stirs its misgivings. This can compound the risk of it overreacting.

At the same time, the failings and insecurities of Western governments, both globalist and non-globalist, inflate the potential for accidental confrontations. Western elites that lack assured values, clear direction and courage are prone to taking arbitrary and shortsighted actions that could escalate out of control.

The respective weaknesses of Western regimes and China could spark greater instability. Western governmental China-bashing is a symptom and intensifier of this incendiary mix. Western aggression, rhetorically and practically, is likely to be answered by firmer Chinese actions. Even if initiated as 'defensive' measures, these can soon morph into offensive measures – and will certainly be perceived as such.

In this way, louder Western predictions about China becoming more aggressive abroad could become self-fulfilling. Subsequent anticipation of having to deal with a militarised crisis leads to preparing for one. And preparing for a militarised crisis brings it closer to reality. This is where the China-bashers could lead us.

23 JUNE 2020

WHY I SIGNED THE HARPER'S LETTER

WENDY KAMINER

'I rest my case', I'm tempted to say, reviewing the unhinged responses of cancel-culture fans intent on cancelling the judicious defence of free speech in our 'Letter on Justice and Open Debate', published by *Harper's* this week. I signed emphatically, which makes me one of 'the worst people in the world of public intellectualism', according to *In These Times*. What's so bad about defending 'the free exchange of information and ideas' and critiquing 'intolerance for opposing views' and 'a vogue for public shaming and ostracism'? In doing so we were not really defending the right to debate and criticise, according to *In These Times*: we were trying to squelch debate and censor our own critics, exhibiting a 'bizarre aversion to being argued against ... [that] now borders on the pathological'.

This is what citizens of cancel culture have apparently learned from Donald Trump: confound your critics by accusing them of precisely the sins you're busy committing. Social-justice warriors have long demanded protection from the 'trauma' of hearing speech they deem offensive, calling for suppression of the speech and shunning of the speaker. So, employing Trumpian tactics, they accuse free-speech advocates of the censoriousness and psychic fragility that's the *raison d'être* of their movement.

I hesitate to condemn this as a bad-faith argument, however perverse, because I suspect that it's often offered sincerely. For years now, progressive censors have characterised free speech as a zero-sum game, claiming that when presumptively privileged people speak, they silence the presumptively oppressed. Civil libertarians hold the contrary (historically vindicated) view that free speech is essential to social change. Or as our letter opined: 'The restriction of debate, whether by a repressive government or an intolerant society, invariably hurts those who lack power and makes everyone less capable of democratic participation.' This should be blindingly obvious in the wake of massive Black Lives Matter protests. Still, for some progressives, it is an article of faith that the defence of free speech is simply another form of censorship.

You can't employ logic against faith, which is why censors are right about this: our battles over free speech, like our battles over abortion rights, are power struggles, not debates. They're shaped by fundamentally conflicting values. 'I support free speech, but ...' is no longer the mantra of people who aim to censor allegedly hateful speech. Now they openly deride free speech and its 'privileged' defenders, as attacks on the 'Justice and Open Debate' letter show. It's 'fatuous, self-important drivel', one critic sneers.

Given the power of cancel culture, it's not surprising that at least two signatories, Kerri K Greenidge and Jennifer Finney Boylan, have now disavowed the letter. There is apparently some dispute over whether Greenidge ever endorsed it, but Finney Boylan acknowledged doing so and apologised for her error, rather pathetically. She signed it partly in the belief that she'd be in the 'good company' of 'Chomsky, Steinem, and Atwood'. She took it back upon finding herself in what many consider bad company. (The much-maligned JK Rowling is a signatory.) In other words, after apparently seeking virtue by association, Finney Boylan found herself saddled with associational guilt.

I saw only a partial list of signatories when I agreed to sign and didn't pay it much attention. I focused on the text, not the names endorsing it. I'm not responsible for their views (which I don't always share), and they're not responsible for mine. The refusal to endorse a statement you support and consider important because it will be endorsed by people with whom you sometimes differ reflects the intolerance for debate that the letter addresses.

I disagree with many of *spiked*'s writers, for example, and they, no doubt, disagree often with me, but in my view that's what makes *spiked* interesting. I have no desire to speak only with or to people who applaud me.

Nor have I ever found disagreement or offensive speech traumatising. And I've been called worse than 'one of the worst people in the world of public intellectualism'. A former colleague on the American Civil Liberties Union national board once called me a 'fucked-out boozy bitch', suggesting that I 'fuck off and die' for criticising the organisation's leadership. He also championed a civility code for the board aimed at squelching dissent.

'Free speech for me, but not for thee', he might have said, echoing the late, great Nat Hentoff's sardonic characterisation of popular approaches to speech, left and right. Rest our case? An unflinching civil libertarian, Hentoff knew that the defence of free speech never rests.

10 JULY 2020

COPYRIGHT © WENDY KAMINER 2020

WHY THE LEFT LOVES CANCEL CULTURE

TOM SLATER

Being left-wing used to mean agitating *against* people losing their jobs. How quaint that feels now. In the culture wars of today, the illiberal left's primary response to any statement it disagrees with seems to be demanding that the person who said it be immediately sacked and made an example of.

For all these people's blather about 'Karens' — that insufferable meme about entitled lower-middle-class white women who always want to speak to the manager — the ultimate Karens today are to be found on the identitarian left. They'll go straight to the manager of anyone who dares utter a dissenting thought.

Now their censoriousness is being 'called out', as they might say. A letter published in *Harper's* last week, signed by a diverse group of liberals, civil libertarians and left-wingers, raised the alarm about the growing intolerance on the left and the mobbing of the insufficiently woke.

The response from the pro-censorship left has been a carnival of obfuscation, bullshit and bad faith. A rogues' gallery of illiberal midwits — many of them veterans of cancellation campaigns themselves — have denied cancel culture is even a thing and valiantly argued with caricatures of their opponents' arguments.

Corbynista *Guardian* columnist Owen Jones says cancel culture is just 'public figures being criticised on Twitter for things they've said'. Here he is apparently struggling with the distinction between 'being criticised' and 'being faced by demands they be sacked', which is of course what we're actually talking about.

That he doesn't seem to know the difference is a little odd, given he spends a good chunk of his time doing the latter nowadays. A few weeks before the *Harper's* letter was published, Jones was calling on Oxford University to fire its deputy director of external affairs and international strategy over something unpleasant he tweeted about TV pundit Ash Sarkar.

This braindead take, that the backlash to cancel culture is just rich people complaining about being criticised, has been repeated *ad nauseam*. Nesrine Malik, of the *Guardian* (again), accused those behind the *Harper's* letter of being influential people 'unaccustomed to being questioned'.

Given the letter was signed by Salman Rushdie, that take doesn't even hold water if you glance at the list of signatories – unless you think the fatwa was a strongly worded letter or a devastating Twitter thread. But nor does it hold water if you bother to read the text itself.

The letter describes 'an intolerance of opposing views' and a 'vogue for public shaming and ostracism' that is leading people to 'fear for their livelihoods if they depart from the consensus', or even just make 'clumsy mistakes'. In the UK, this culture has resulted in much more than 'criticism' of dubious public figures.

Indeed, even upstanding people in public life, like Nobel Prize-winning scientist Sir Tim Hunt and veteran newsreader Alastair Stewart, have been sacked after their innocent words were yanked out of context and their employers gave in to mob pressure.

But, more importantly, the letter argues that this culture is more of a threat to those *without* power, influence and gilded academic positions. 'The restriction of debate, whether by a repressive government or an intolerant society', it says, 'invariably hurts those who lack power and makes everyone less capable of democratic participation'.

This is a crucial point. The mobbing of prominent figures doesn't only have a chilling effect on debate more broadly, by setting the terms of acceptable debate for everyone else; it also legitimises the cancellation of less powerful people – those less able to fight back.

Critics of the *Harper's* letter constantly single out one of its signatories – JK Rowling, who has faced abuse and death and rape threats for expressing trans-sceptical views. The idea that this multimillionaire author, with more than 14million Twitter followers, has been 'silenced' is ridiculous, they scoff.

But no one, including Rowling herself, is saying that she has been silenced or cancelled. Rather, it is the people further down the pecking order, those without hundreds of millions of pounds in the bank, who will ultimately bear the brunt of this silencing dynamic.

In fact, in relation to the Rowling controversy, that has already happened. Children's author Gillian Philip was sacked in July for the crime of expressing support for JK Rowling. After 24 hours of abuse and complaints, her publisher dumped her.

This case was put to activist and songwriter Billy Bragg on Twitter, after he rubbished cancel culture in the *Guardian* (and again). In response, this alleged socialist declared: 'I believe that employers have a right to act in such circumstances.'

Here, Bragg just came clean about what illiberal leftists often try to obscure — that they have become so intolerant that they now stick up for the right of employers to sack people for their opinions. In this culture war, 'bosses' rights' is their rallying cry.

While woke leftists' cancelling efforts are most often aimed at people in the more rarefied circles — the media, academia, the arts — that they move in, the climate they have whipped up will inevitably hit ordinary working people, too.

Brian Leach, a disabled grandfather, lost his job in an Asda store in Yorkshire in 2019 after he shared a Billy Connolly routine, which took the piss out of jihadists, on his personal Facebook page. Someone else on staff took offence, and he was sacked.

That the bourgeois left has become increasingly shrill and intolerant has been clear for some time. But it's still worth asking why these supposed radicals are so comfortable handing over the power to police speech to the state, bosses and Silicon Valley.

Part of it has to do with their distance from working people. This is now so vast that they have begun to see woke corporations as the agents of change and pretty widely held beliefs — like thinking that rushing to put kids on puberty-blockers is probably not a good idea — as unspeakable heresies.

But it also speaks to how fundamentally unthreatening their own ideas are. On cultural matters, certainly, they *are* the establishment — their kooky views on gender, privilege and much else besides are not only shared but also enforced by the state and Silicon Valley.

Meanwhile, their sixth-formerish poseur socialism isn't a threat to anyone, not least because it lacks any popular support. Indeed, five years of Owen Jones-ism running the Labour Party led to it handing over its northern working-class heartlands to the Tories at the last election.

Now, deeply disappointed with ordinary people, the bourgeois left has resigned itself to policing their opinions, doing by compulsion and censure what it cannot do by reason and argument, with the assistance of the capitalist class where necessary.

No wonder these activists cling to cancel culture. It is all they've got left. In a way, it is all a bit tragic. But it is also a menace to the free speech of precisely the people the left once aspired to represent.

13 JULY 2020

LET'S ABOLISH RACE

INAYA FOLARIN IMAN

Thanks to the rise of identity politics and growing political polarisation, the politics of race has come to play an increasingly important role in mainstream public life over the past decade. The issues of race and racism now dominate the national conversation.

However, at the same time there is a growing opposition to the politics of race. Some writers and thinkers, like Kmele Foster and Thomas Chatterton Williams, are seeking to redirect the conversation about race. They don't want simply to oppose racism, or to critique identity politics. They want to do away with the notion of race altogether. Their rallying cry is, 'abolish race'.

Race abolitionism poses a challenge to both racism and modern forms of 'anti-racism'. It holds that the social construct of race is based on a taxonomy invented to create and reinforce racial hierarchies. Therefore, to continue to affirm the meaning and existence of race will inevitably perpetuate racial hierarchies.

The concept of 'race' is scientifically and socially unsupportable. Unlike 'sex', which describes the material reality of the divided reproductive function of a given species, the concept of race has no such material, biological basis. That's why its meaning is constantly shifting. For example, 'mixed race' people often consider themselves to be black, and at one time in the not too distant past, all non-white people were considered black. At the same time, several groups of people who we now consider to be unquestionably 'white' (for example, the Irish or Italians) were once regarded as less than totally 'white'.

The perpetuation of the notion of race is in direct opposition to humanism and universalism. By dividing human beings into broad racialised categories, and institutionalising those categories in the form of quotas, 'positive discrimination' schemes, 'black-only' spaces and so on, identitarians reify race and racialise social life.

Leftist identitarians are fond of talking of human attributes as 'social constructs'. However, their use of social-constructionist ideas is less radical than it sounds. In terms of race, they suggest that merely inverting racial hierarchies is sufficient to achieve social justice. So, instead of 'whiteness' being constructed to connote purity, power and intelligence, activists seek to invert its meaning so that it connotes guilt, debasement and privilege. Likewise, with 'blackness', activists seek to imbue it with new meanings, from innocence to moral superiority.

These tactics do not challenge racism, however. They preserve it, because they fail to challenge the idea of race itself. This raises several related questions. What does it mean to challenge the idea of race? What does it entail for a person to refuse to accept his or her racial designation? And, ultimately, what does abolishing race mean in practical terms?

Well, first, it means recognising that racial essentialism is a destructive idea, regardless of where it is coming from on the political spectrum. This concept assumes that individuals can be reduced to some racial essence, which in turn determines how they ought to behave and act. Thus, we need to deconstruct the idea of race, to de-essentialise or de-naturalise it. In doing so, individuals will become a little more free to be themselves, rather than to live as their racial identity dictates.

Historically, social progress has been won through precisely such challenges to determinism, be it biological or, in this case, cultural. Think, for example, of feminists' challenge to the idea of what it is to be a woman. Such challenges rest, in part, on what existentialists used to refer to as the 'transcendental' elements to our existence – that is to say, our existence precedes our essence. We therefore do not have to be defined by the designations (or indeed identities) imposed upon us. This includes not just the designations of racists, but those of anti-racists, too.

This is not easy. Race presents itself as such an eternal and omnipresent category of identity that many people today cannot imagine themselves existing outside of the racialised categories ascribed to them from birth, which proceed to determine their social relations. Because of this, the abolition of race is a radical challenge to the status quo. It poses the question of what possibilities for human relationships exist beyond the boundary of race. How can we destabilise the ideology and belief system of race?

It is time for us to think imaginatively about what the abolition of race might mean for us as individuals, and for society as a whole. Abolishing race doesn't mean that we should ignore racism, however. It simply means that we should refuse to instil race with meaning – positive or negative.

Those on the identitarian left who currently want to re-essentialise the concept of 'race' have no positive vision beyond demanding recognition for past or imagined grievances. This is a dismal vision of our future possibilities as a unified humanity. It can only be challenged when we forge a new collective vision, one based on the values of freedom, humanism and universalism.

4 AUGUST 2020

WOKE CLASS HATRED

TOM SLATER

In the latest expression of its apparent death wish, the BBC has put out a clip on social media of psychologist and former NBA player John Amaechi waxing lyrical on the subject of white privilege. In it, he gently explains why white privilege is real, and is even enjoyed by the underprivileged whites who generally resent the idea.

This is not the only time of late that the BBC – faced with accusations of bias and campaigns to defund it – appeared to troll its critics. A podcast clip of two middle-class white women accusing other middle-class white women of being racist 'Karens' also lit up the BBC complaints page recently.

But that Amaechi's little video was put out on BBC Bitesize, the corporation's homework and revision site, seemed particularly cheeky. That teenagers can now get woke on the same site as they revise for their French GCSE shows how orthodox ideas around identity politics and privilege have become at the BBC – and at elite institutions in general.

There was no debate set up here; the other side of this contentious issue was not given an airing. The theory of white privilege, it seems, is considered by the Beeb to be as uncontroversial as saying that we went to war in 1939 or that Henry VIII had six wives – just another plain fact to be relayed to the young folk.

Across the Atlantic, it fell to billionaire Oprah Winfrey to throw a hand grenade into this particularly tense arena of the culture war. On her Apple TV+ show, *The Oprah Conversation*, she recently said that even poor white people enjoy white privilege.

'There are white people who are not as powerful', the media mogul, net worth $2.6 billion, graciously conceded. 'But they still, no matter where they are on the rung or ladder of success, they still have their whiteness.' Right-wing Twitter had a field day, mocking the absurdity of a billionaire lecturing poor people about the privilege they enjoy.

Indeed, one of the consequences of the left's increasing obsession with identity politics is that it has ceded the language of class to the right. The black Tory mayoral candidate for London, Shaun Bailey, said in a recent speech that he had more in common with a white kid from Dagenham than a black kid from Hampstead, an old left-wing formulation about class solidarity.

What some right-wingers are cottoning on to, and exploiting to varying degrees of electoral success (Bailey, bless him, doesn't stand a chance), is that the left's recent embrace of wokeness is fundamentally a betrayal of class politics, and that where class politics can unite, wittering on about privilege only divides.

On a practical level, identity politics is just bad politics. Telling working-class white people, a huge chunk of the electorate, that even if they're struggling to pay the bills and are thousands of pounds in debt they should always remember it could be worse is, at best, a non-starter. Making statements like 'you can be homeless and still have white privilege' – as model, trans activist and one-time Labour adviser Munroe Bergdorf did a few years back – would be churlish, to put it lightly, even if they were true.

But the problem with the theory of white privilege is not just that it winds people up. It also fundamentally fails to explain inequalities in society. In the UK, white working-class boys are the poorest performing group in terms of educational attainment. Unless we are expected to believe this is solely down to them squandering their relative privilege, clearly race isn't everything.

This is not to say racism doesn't exist, or that racial inequalities aren't real and serious. But the picture is far more complicated than the narrative of 'white privilege' would have us believe. British workers of Chinese and Indian heritage are among the highest-earning ethnic groups by hourly pay, far outperforming white Brits. There are also significant gaps in educational attainment between British African and British Caribbean kids, suggesting race alone cannot explain everything.

For all the disparities in outcomes between different groups, influenced by various cultural, historical and economic factors, what class you were born into remains far more significant than your skin colour. Even in eras far more racist and discriminatory than our own, radicals recognised that overcoming class domination went hand-in-hand with overcoming racism – not least given many ethnic minorities were and are disproportionately working class.

Simplistic notions like white privilege, then, obfuscate issues of economic privilege and dim the prospects of forging the coalitions necessary to make life better for all working people. What's more, among the liberal middle classes, identity politics appears to have rehabilitated a form of class hatred, with the white working-class forever the implied villain of the piece.

After Black Lives Matter protesters toppled the statue of slave trader Edward Colston in Bristol in June, someone erected a temporary statue near the plinth, depicting a fat, string-vest-wearing pleb sitting in a wheelie bin and staring at his phone screen, on which were the words 'England for the English'. Today, a white working-class caricature is what many associate with racism.

Regrettably, modern anti-racism has become the means through which class hatred is peddled and inflamed. Indeed, research suggests that 'white privilege' training has no impact on social liberals' sympathy towards black people, but it does decrease their sympathy towards poor whites, leaving them more likely to think poor whites have 'failed to take advantage of their racial privilege'.

Left-wing identity politics claims to sit in the anti-racist tradition. But today it plays much the same role that the racist right did in the past. It works to fracture class solidarity by insisting that different sections of the working class are fundamentally antagonistic to one another's interests.

No wonder the elites love this 'white privilege' guff so much. A divided working class is no threat to them.

7 AUGUST 2020

AUSTRALIA'S COVID AUTOCRACY

NICK CATER

The pandemic is revealing more uncomfortable truths by the day, like our willingness to abandon our freedoms and traditions at the first whiff of grapeshot.

Governments mistrustful of citizens have been too quick to respond to risks to public health with coercion, rather than simply appealing for a civic-minded people to do the right thing.

In Australia there has been a level of official control seldom seen since the convict era. There has been barely any opposition. A nation once prepared to make the ultimate sacrifice of lives in defence of liberty is surrendering its freedom on the pretext of saving lives.

We are learning that when we dispense with the checks and balances that make democratic governments better than they otherwise might be, there is an exponential increase in the number and scale of state-induced blunders.

Exhibit A is the state of Victoria, where Covid-19 has recently spread through the community in what might be called a second wave if there had been a first wave, which there wasn't.

When Britain, the US and much of Europe were struggling with mass outbreaks in April, Australia and New Zealand had the virus under control thanks largely to the prompt closure of borders.

It might have stayed that way but for a breach of quarantine security in Melbourne, where inadequate supervision of returning Australians in hotel quarantine allowed infected people to escape.

The loss of life in Australia has so far been slight compared with America or Britain. Yet the elevated risk was enough for Victoria's premier, Dan Andrews, to declare a 'state of disaster' for only the second time in Victoria's history. Andrews, incidentally, was responsible for declaring both of them.

Victoria became an autocracy overnight, granting unfettered power to a premier unaccountable to parliament and freed from the rule of law. The police have turned from citizens in uniform to the enforcers of ministerial declarations, most of them quite absurd.

Melbourne has become the first city in Australia to fall under a curfew. Andrews' predecessors felt no need for one during the First World War, Second World War, the Spanish Flu pandemic or the 1923 police strike when violent mobs rampaged through the city and overturned a tram.

Yet the outbreak of a virus from China that currently kills a small proportion of those it affects in the general population, and a negligible percentage of people below retirement age, was considered grave enough to suspend democracy and the rule of law.

The bridge over the River Murray on the Hume Highway, linking the Victorian city of Wodonga and Albury in New South Wales, has become Australia's Checkpoint Charlie, the free world on one side and tyranny on the other.

Those tempted to swim across should know that police and army reservists are patrolling the Murray's northern banks assisted by helicopters and drones. Up to six months in jail awaits those without papers.

Melbourne residents who leave their homes between 8pm and 5am face a $5,000 fine, imposed by police not the courts. Fines will also be issued to anyone who is caught without a mask, exercises for more than an hour, wanders further than 5km from home, goes fishing or plays golf, among other things.

Like the villain in a dystopian novel, Victoria's democratically elected premier is interfering with citizen's private lives in a manner most will have imagined impossible in a nation settled by the heirs of Magna Carta.

In his masterful book on the Anglosphere, Dan Hannan praised Australia as a country where the libertarian philosophy of John Stuart Mill was made flesh. Hannan might care to revisit that bit, as Victoria breaks record after record in the contest of illiberalism, employing all the available instruments of modern surveillance to keep its citizens in check.

If the premier and his officials know how many cases of infection can be tolerated they are keeping it from the citizens. No one knows how long the lockdown measures will end or what comes next.

The consequences for the Victorian economy, which accounts for a quarter of Australia's GDP, are growing exponentially. The price of shutting down business today is the loss of future opportunity. The effects of this recession will be felt for a generation at least. The most deadly effects of the virus may be reserved for the elderly and sickly, but the biggest losers will be those in the prime of their life.

Much of what we are losing cannot be counted in dollars and cents. Freedoms, once surrendered, can be impossible to recover.

The assumption of emergency powers to fight a real or exaggerated threat is the oldest trick in the manual of despotism. Countries ruled by tyranny are frequently those from which millions long to flee, just as they do in Victoria right now, if only for a holiday.

The erosion of democracies typically begins with the indefinite suspension of parliament, as the Victorian state parliament has been.

Autocrats are drawn to centrally planned economies, with the inevitable mismatch of supply and demand. Residents of Victoria, the food bowl of Australia, face shortages of meat and other essentials and the prospect of rationing for the first time since the Second World War.

Autocracies are notorious for the proliferation of permits and the checking of papers. In Victoria, a permit is required to travel, work or cross the border. Military personnel are being used as auxiliary police, police powers have been drastically increased and punitive fines introduced.

Citizens are encouraged to act as informants against their employer and also neighbours.

There has not been one guarantee that all or any of these crackdown laws will be repealed.

Those who grew up with pride in their country and its part in overcoming the great 20th-century tyrannies are understandably shocked at how much we appear willing to surrender for benefits that are as yet unspecified.

We shouldn't be surprised at the tacit compliance of the media, which, by and large, have not seen fit to challenge the measures. Journalists, like some politicians, have a professional interest in exaggerating the threat. 'All quiet on the Covid-19 front' is not a story worthy of page one.

With time, the Andrews administration's draconian and illiberal stage-four lockdown will come to be seen as a monstrous administrative mistake that has compounded the effects of the blunders that allowed the virus to run wild.

Let's hope at least that the lockdown slows the general rate of infection, since the government seems incapable of protecting nursing-home residents any other way.

Even if it does, we are bound to ask if the result was worth the months that will have been added to the recession, the swelling of the ranks of the long-term unemployed, and the freedoms citizens have been forced to relinquish, with no guarantee they will get them back.

13 AUGUST 2020

ISLAMISM IS NOT A MENTAL ILLNESS

SABINE BEPPLER-SPAHL

On the night it happened, I could hear ambulances in Berlin-Tempelhof where I live. Just a few kilometres away on the motor-way, a 30-year-old Iraqi – a former refugee who is believed to have arrived in Germany in 2016 – had been ramming motorcyclists with his car, leaving six people injured, some of them seriously. One of them, a fireman on his way back from work, suffered life-threatening injuries.

The attacker stopped on the motorway and shouted 'Allahu Akbar' as he got out of his car. He then got out a prayer mat and began to pray in the middle of the road. When he was finally overwhelmed by two policemen, he pointed to a box that he had placed on his car roof, claiming it contained a bomb, though it later transpired that it was a toolbox.

Most observers, including Berlin's senator for interior affairs, Andreas Geisel, rightly said that the incident was a chilling reminder of the ongoing threat posed by Islamist terrorism. Yet not long after the incident, the tone of the debate quickly changed.

The focus increasingly shifted to the mental state of the perpetrator. There were 'indications of mental instability', according to prosecutors. Picking up on this, liberal newspaper *taz* quoted a doctor who claimed that it was wrong even to speak of Islamist terror. He argued that if the man had already been treated for psychological problems, and was not yet known to have been involved in an Islamist group, then one couldn't blame the attack on Islamist terrorism.

It is indeed hard to believe that anyone who deliberately tried to kill motorcyclists, and put out a prayer mat in the middle of the motorway, wasn't out of his mind in some way. But claiming that the attack was not Islamist in nature seems bizarre. For one thing, it simply ignores the clear Islamist elements. It also presents radicalisation as an almost entirely psychological phenomenon. It ignores the wider political and social context of this type of terrorism. Worse still, it presents its perpetrators as vulnerable victims.

As mad as the attacker may have been, he was still conscious – or zealous – enough to have embraced a jihadist worldview. For instance, he referred to himself as a martyr on his Facebook page in a post made just hours before the attack. The idea that he wasn't part of a wider Islamic network also seems unlikely to be true, as he reportedly got plenty of likes for his post.

It is highly doubtful that the people who are now claiming the incident had nothing to do with radical Islamism would say the same thing about a similar attack by suspected neo-Nazis. Following a horrendous shooting of mainly Turkish people in a shisha bar in Hanau in February, which killed 10 people, *taz* responded very differently. 'Terrorists are mostly not ill', was the headline of a piece in which a psychiatrist explained that 'the killer was mentally ill, but his act nonetheless clearly followed a right-wing extremist narrative'.

This difference in approach to both acts of terrorism has nothing to do with the number of victims – the Islamist Berlin attacker may not have had a gun or a bomb, but he was just as interested in killing as many innocent people as possible as the right-wing Hanau attacker was. The problem is cultural. While most commentators have no problem with calling on society to stand together against the far right, they are more reluctant to do so in relation to militant Islam.

After years of presenting tolerance of Islam as a central component of a liberal, multicultural society, many seem to find it hard to acknowledge that not all manifestations of Islam are good. The result is that criticism of radical Islam has largely become the preserve of far-right groups such as Pegida. But the reluctance to condemn Islamist terrorism, and the refusal to see it for what it is, needs to stop.

Viewing Islamist terrorists as mainly 'mad', or even as victims of circumstance, almost inevitably leads either to cynicism or to a sense of fatalism within society at large. Radical jihadism is a vicious ideology that has inspired countless evil deeds. It is time for society to stand together against it.

25 AUGUST 2020

THE BLACK LIVES WE DON'T TALK ABOUT

LUKE GITTOS

The names Jacob Blake, George Floyd, Trayvon Martin and Mark Duggan have become known across the globe as victims of police brutality. But consider another list: Jeremy Meneses-Chalarca, Louis Johnson and Babacar Diagne. These young men, all from black and ethnic-minority backgrounds, were killed in the most appalling circumstances, yet most people will not know who they are. They do not figure in our discussion of 'black lives'. These are just three of the young men who have died this year in Britain as a result of knife violence.

All of the murders were appalling. The killing of Jeremy Meneses-Chalarca, whose mother was from Colombia, occurred at 5.30pm on Oxford Street. It was watched by 'many witnesses', according to reports. Jeremy, who had turned 17 in July, was stabbed to death by another teenager in the middle of one of London's busiest shopping streets. It barely made the news.

Louis Johnson was stabbed at East Croydon railway station, in front of commuters. Johnson complained to his friends on the morning of his killing that he had 'been in a scuffle' with a stranger, and he feared he had a 'target on his back'. A 17-year-old boy has been convicted of Johnson's murder. It appears the two had an ongoing feud.

Babacar Diagne was just 15 at the time of his death. He was found dead on grassland in Coventry. Three boys were later charged with his murder. During the investigation 11 people were arrested, including a 15-year-old girl who was arrested on suspicion of conspiracy to commit murder. The motive for the attack remains unclear. Again, it was barely reported.

What is striking about so many killings today is how brazen they are. Andre Bent, 21, was murdered in 2019 during a mass brawl in front of a nightclub, following a performance by rapper MoStack. The person who filmed the killing can be heard laughing and mocking Bent as he is being stabbed. This year, Enroy Ruddock boasted over Snapchat about allegedly murdering 21-year-old Emmanuel Lukenga. The murder of Karl Gallagher in Smethwick in April this year was captured on film and widely circulated. Much of this violence is happening out in the open, often in the middle of the day, where members of the public are able to capture the killings on camera.

These young men, who are all from ethnic-minority backgrounds, simply don't figure in the debate around Black Lives Matter. On the rare occasions these deaths are discussed, we only ever hear predictable arguments on two sides of a culture war. One side blames absentee fathers and 'cultural factors' like violent music. The other side blames economic degradation and cuts to youth services. The men and boys who die in these incidents simply fall into the background.

Stuart Hall had a name for the young men who died in British custody suites during the 1970s. He described how the liberal majority viewed these men as 'ragamuffins' who most likely deserved their treatment by the police. Their deaths did not cause significant outrage because they were easily dismissed as troublemakers. The specifics of the deaths went undiscussed. They were not worthy of moral consideration.

Today, it is the victims of knife crime who are society's 'ragamuffins'. They are ignored by the BLM movement because they do not fit easily into a narrative of victimhood. We cannot talk about their killings, their lives, their motivations or their backgrounds.

The lack of discussion has led to deep confusion about why these men are dying. Shaun Bailey, the Conservative candidate for mayor of London, argues that companies should be forced to carry out drug tests on their employees to help slow the drug trade. He assumes this would, in turn, help combat the knife-crime problem. But many of the deaths in our cities have nothing to do with dealing cocaine to middle-class households. Many knife attacks appear to be motivated mainly by minor social disputes and social-media 'beefs' that spiral out of control.

Commentators are reluctant to address the most disturbing specifics of today's violence. Author and rapper Akala is typical in this regard. He went viral with his views on youth violence in 2019. His argument is that: 'The social indicators for serious youth violence have remained identical for almost 200 years ... poverty, domestic abuse, lack of education – expulsion from school.' He says almost half the people in prison today in Britain were expelled from school as children, compared with just one per cent of the population as a whole. Akala has some good points to make. But the view that youth violence is all down to 'social indicators' – a view shared by a number of commentators – creates confusion rather than clarity.

First, the picture is far more complicated. Home Office research into serious violence from July 2019 analysed the indicators found to be significantly associated with weapon carrying and use at the age of 14. Important factors included gender, the number of siblings in a particular household, the onset of puberty and the frequency of truanting.

The report then analysed the indicators found to be significantly associated with 'serious violence-linked behaviours' (SVLB), which were self-reported at age 18. This found that 'child maltreatment' was a significant factor. So was the 'father's marital status'. Interestingly, the number of siblings in a household was more significant in leading to SVLB than many other household-related factors. As the report puts it, 'those with no siblings and those with four or more siblings were generally more likely to report weapon carrying / use than those with one sibling'.

The report also suggested that truancy was a more significant indicator of weapon carrying and use than school exclusion. An earlier Home Office paper from 2015 on gang and youth violence similarly found that 'running away and truancy' were strong risk factors for youth violence. This earlier report contained an additional finding that is rarely talked about: 'Across the age groups, *individual factors* (such as low self-esteem) as opposed to their contexts (such as coming from a low-income family) are found to be the most powerful signs of risk.' In other words, individual traits and decisions are better indications of a young person's risk of being involved in serious violence than what we might call 'social indicators'. In this vein, it is interesting to note that Akala and others focus on exclusion rather than truancy. This reflects a desire to deny the agency of those involved in knife crime.

Of course, these Home Office reports do not give the full picture. We should not rely on them to dictate our approach to solving serious youth violence. But it is also important to understand what we do and do not know. I am happy to be corrected, but I have not found any serious evidence to support the claim that the relevant social indicators have 'remained identical across 200 years', as Akala argues. After all, it is hard to see how something like exclusion from school could be an indicator of youth violence in both the 19th and 21st centuries, given that much of the population 200 years ago did not attend school.

The impulse of many commentators is to ignore what is specific about today's killings. They would rather focus on the abstract factors that provide continuity between the violence that occurred between, say, the Mods and Rockers on Brighton beach in the 1960s and the young men on London's council estates today.

Akala's policy prescription is one-word long: Glasgow. The 'holistic approach' adopted in Scotland led to a rapid decline in serious youth violence, he argues. 'Intervening early' with counselling, good jobs and youth services is the best solution. He is not alone in venerating Glasgow. This 'public-health approach' is often held up as 'what we should do' about knife crime. But it is not all that it seems.

Glasgow's 'holistic approach' generally refers to the establishment of the Violence Reduction Unit in 2005. Since then, the VRU has been providing mentoring and employment opportunities to gang members and running educational sessions in schools.

The VRU is hardly unique in offering state-sponsored mentoring and employment opportunities to young people. But more importantly, Glasgow's reforms were not as benign as they are often presented. By 2010, stop-and-search rates in Scotland were around four times higher than in England and Wales. Seventy per cent of recorded searches were undertaken without reasonable suspicion. Scotland also introduced sentencing guidelines in 2016 that allowed those carrying knives to be jailed for five years.

While the maximum sentence was only handed out very rarely, the average prison sentence for knife possession also increased by around 85 per cent between 2008 and 2018.

The appeal of this public-health approach is that it allows us to continue to treat young men as a problem to be managed, rather than as moral agents. Judges in murder trials routinely refer to the 'law of the jungle' when describing the environments in which these killings occur, as though they are happening somewhere far away from the streets of our major cities. Academics and commentators refer to a 'gang culture' in which otherwise appalling behaviour can be, in some respects, rationalised. These are attempts to treat young ethnic-minority men as though they live in a separate moral community to the rest of us. Those who refer to 'gang culture' are often making well-meaning attempts to explain inexplicable behaviour. But the effect is to exacerbate the feeling among these men that they are, in some sense, exiles from the society around them. A refusal to discuss the details of these killings reflects a culture of low expectations, which almost expects that young black men will carry on murdering each other.

This problem is exacerbated by the tendency to see young ethnic-minority men as heavily victimised by wider society. While many of these men do suffer from material deprivation, we should also recognise that a narrative of victimhood can provide this violence with an implicit justification. If young men are told to believe that all of society is geared against them, it is not hard to see how this can cultivate a sense of grievance that has the potential to translate into serious violence. There can be little motivation to obey the laws of a society that you believe has been built to keep you down.

It is also worth considering how these killings reflect the profound importance placed on individual self-esteem by wider society. The fact that so many of these killings arise from social-media spats and social disagreements suggests that these men take their self-esteem and reputations very seriously. They are hardly alone in this. Today's therapeutic culture continually reminds us that our sense of self-worth is essential to a happy life. Perhaps a culture that venerates individual self-worth encourages young men to think that personal slights and knocks to confidence are worth killing for. This also goes some way to explaining the very public and performative nature of many of these attacks.

If we are to understand these killings, we must at least talk about them on their own terms. We have to look seriously at the young men involved. We should recognise that these young killers are not forced to behave the way they do by economic hardship or a lack of youth services. They make choices. Taking this starting point allows us to take these young men seriously, as our fellow citizens, and to confront these crimes head-on. Until we do, young men will continue to die. And their deaths will continue to struggle to make the news.

31 AUGUST 2020

RIOTING OVER A NARRATIVE

WILFRED REILLY

The Democrats didn't talk about the riots.

During the four-day Democratic National Convention, which ran from 17 to 20 August, virtually no primetime speakers discussed the nationwide violence that followed the horrific death of George Floyd while restrained by Minneapolis police. Andrew Cuomo discussed his widely praised fight against the coronavirus epidemic – although New York led the nation in Covid-19 deaths – but not the street-fighting or looting. Bill Clinton praised Joe Biden and brought back memories of his own glory years, discussing how a proper president should use the Oval Office, while Hillary Clinton touched on why her own tenure in the Oval never occurred. Barack Obama harshly but non-specifically criticised the current lead occupant of the White House, while Uncle Joe himself told us that he was Jill Biden's husband. About Minneapolis or Atlanta or Portland – Kenosha hadn't happened yet – basically nada.

This was an astonishing omission, akin to the upper-executive team of General Motors not mentioning 'automobiles' during an annual meeting. Since the death of George Floyd, the US has been roiled by probably the most devastating series of widespread urban riots since 1968's 'Summer of Love / Rage'. According to reports, at least 30 people have so far been killed during the violence, with 900 law-enforcement officers and an unknown number of rioters and protesters hospitalised, 14,000 people arrested, and billions of dollars in property damage done.

A list of the businesses so far damaged or destroyed in Minneapolis, where rioting began, runs into the hundreds – and includes all too many minority-owned and urban-chic establishments. In the same

city, rioters literally burned an active police station, torching
the sizeable 3rd Precinct building as officers in uniform retreated
in good order.

In addition to 'sympathetic' protests and riots in honour of
Floyd in many cities, secondary waves of violence have followed
the deaths of other black men at the hands of police. In Atlanta,
the death of Rayshard Brooks led to the burning of a franchise fast-
food restaurant, and several days of sharp violence between activists
and police. In Chicago, a rumour that a 15-year-old male had been
shot by police led to the looting of significant chunks of the legendary
Magnificent Mile, and to mayor Lori Lightfoot literally ordering
the access bridges to the city centre to be raised, *Batman Begins*-style.
Similarly, if less dramatically, significant violence followed the
Detroit shooting of Hakim Littleton. Riots began in Kenosha after a
man named Jacob Blake was shot seven times in the back by police.

There are several interesting and empirically relevant
characteristics of these riots. First, while the George Floyd video,
for example, is genuinely upsetting to watch, the riots are based
around a narrative that is simply not empirically true. There is
no ongoing race war in the United States, and black people are
not being murdered in large numbers by the police. Inter-racial
violent crime involving blacks and whites is around five per cent
of crime in a typical year, and black people generally commit roughly
80 per cent of it. This is not necessarily even surprising, given that
there are more whites and they have more money, but it does not
indicate a near-genocide. Statistics like these can be confirmed
simply by taking a look at the annual Bureau of Justice Statistics
National Crime Report. In the arena specifically of police violence,
the total number of unarmed black men shot by law-enforcement
officers in the most recent year on record was 14.

Moving from broad generalities to specifics, many of the
individual cases that prompted rioting collapse under serious
analysis. The '15-year-old boy' whose death caused the Chicago
riots turned out to be a 20-year-old man. He was shooting at police
when he got shot. And he is still alive. The Detroit policing 'victim',
Hakim Littleton, was also involved in a literal gun battle with police.
Rayshard Brooks was also firing at cops, albeit with a police-strength

taser rather than a pistol, when he died. More recently, the Jacob Blake situation also looks to be far more complex than we were originally told. While attorney Benjamin Crump presented Blake as a Good Samaritan, essentially shot at random while attempting to break up a fight between women, we now know that Blake had an active warrant for rape, the police were called specifically to respond to him by a woman who may have been his original victim, and he was shot after a fight and a taser failure — while quite probably going for a large knife.

A second notable fact about the riots is that they seem to be taking place almost entirely where saying what I just did is taboo — in cities run by left-wing Democratic politicians (Portland, Minneapolis, Seattle, Atlanta, DC, Chicago), generally also in states led by Democrats on the left (Minnesota, Oregon, Washington, Illinois, with Georgia as a centre-right outlier). This is a rather remarkable finding. While working-class whites, blacks, Muslim Americans and so forth may (half-)jokingly tease one another about crime rates, the actual fact is that most crime is an ecumenical business. There are exceptions like robbery, but the rolls of those arrested annually for fist-fighting or wife-beating or DUI often 'look like America' in racial and political terms. In contrast, it would be hard to think of a single large conservative city, including quite diverse towns — Oklahoma City, Colorado Springs, Arlington, Omaha, Anaheim — that experienced significant rioting or violence.

Life being multivariate, there are almost certainly many reasons for this. Liberals are much more likely to be critical of law-and-order policing, sometimes justly, than conservatives. However, another key variable seems to be efficacy of leadership. Following riots in Baltimore in 2015, mayor Stephanie Rawlings-Blake said the quiet part out loud, telling reporters, when asked about how police responded to the protests, that 'we also gave those who wished to destroy space to do that as well'. Since then Democratic leaders seeking votes have not infrequently responded to rioting or street-fighting by giving the participants 'room to destroy'.

Portland mayor Ted Wheeler recently responded to a suggestion from President Donald Trump, that National Guard troops be sent to Portland in response to over 90 consecutive days of rioting, by posting a page-long denial letter to his public Twitter account. The letter opened: 'On behalf of the city of Portland: No thanks.' It went on to praise the city's tens of thousands of 'peaceful' protesters and marchers, and closed by saying: 'Stay away, please.' In a horrific example of irony, the letter went live on 28 August – a day later a young man was killed during Portland face-offs between Antifa-style protesters and right-wing group Patriot Prayer.

This brings us to a final twist of the riot story: the frantic attempt by activists and some members of the mainstream media to paint these ugly incidents as somehow the work of Donald Trump, root of all evil, and his supporters. After weeks of quite mainstream pieces with titles like 'In defence of looting', journalists almost universally rediscovered the idea that street mayhem is bad when Kyle Rittenhouse arrived on the scene. A member of a motley crew of right-leaning men who arrived in Kenosha to 'protect property' from rioters and looters, the 17-year-old Rittenhouse shot three other men during what can quite fairly be described as an armed battle in the middle of a public road.

To give only one of literally tens of thousands of similar takes from Twitter and Facebook, Congresswoman Ayanna Pressley referred to Rittenhouse as a 'white-supremacist domestic terrorist' and the pursuers he shot as peaceful folk 'assembled to affirm the value, dignity, and worth of black lives'. Meanwhile, Senator Chris Murphy called him a 'deranged white nationalist Trump supporter' who apparently decided at random to show up at a peaceful protest with a rifle 'and start shooting people'. The same tone pervaded Joe Biden's lengthy statement responding to the shooting of a Trump supporter by an Antifa fighter: he used the occasion to criticise violence on left and right, and to note that 'all of us are less safe because Donald Trump can't do the job'.

While I personally doubt Americans will be persuaded that left-wing riots, in left-wing cities, targeting right-wing institutions are the fault of the right, it remains to be seen how we will react to them. Broadly speaking, there are three responses that I predict and largely support: we will vote, move, and arm up. While not personally stunned by the brilliance of either serious contender in the presidential race, I strongly encourage US citizens to punish all local officials who simply allowed chaos in the streets in the voting booth this fall, and I expect that many will.

A smaller but substantial number of countrymen, motivated both by the spreading violence and by state-wide Covid-19 orders banning such things as funerals with mourners in attendance, are likely to leave mega-cities for smaller towns and even for the more rural 'red' states. Finally, many, many people, including all six of the wokest urban leftists I know, are lining up to buy rifles and shotguns for home defence. While there is certainly a critical conversation to be had about gun culture in the us, the time to have it is not while discussing police defunding amid widespread chaos.

With all that said, a key point is that the ongoing violence not only has predictable responses we can logically expect, but also a predictable end date. While some fighting in the streets will likely continue, I would bet that we can predict to the day when the mass media will tone down the hysterical coverage of every incident of Trump-supporter-on-protester violence, and politicians on all sides will again begin to recognise a kid walking out of a department store with a flat-screen TV as a plain ol' criminal rather than a keen Foucauldian social critic. That day is 4 November 2020.

In the meantime, let's stick together, and hope everyone makes it until then. As a wise Britisher once said: keep calm and carry on.

I SEPTEMBER 2020

WHY 'PUBLIC HEALTH' FAILED

CHRISTOPHER SNOWDON

In June, 1,288 public-health professionals and 'community stakeholders' signed a letter condemning anti-lockdown protesters in the US who were calling for the economy to be reopened. You would expect nothing less. There was a pandemic raging, lockdowns were the law, and their job was to protect public health. And yet the criticism of these protesters was only a prelude to their main point, which was to offer wholehearted support to another group of protesters attending mass gatherings during a pandemic. When it came to the Black Lives Matter protests, they said that 'as public-health advocates, we do not condemn these gatherings as risky for Covid-19 transmission. We support them as vital to the national public health.'

They added: 'We express solidarity and gratitude toward demonstrators who have already taken on enormous personal risk to advocate for their own health, the health of their communities, and the public health of the United States. We pledge our services as allies who share this goal.'

For the avoidance of doubt, they stressed again that: 'This should not be confused with a permissive stance on all gatherings, particularly protests against stay-home orders.'

The signatories clearly believed that mass gatherings of any kind would lead to more infections, hospitalisations and possibly deaths (they advised the government to 'prepare for an increased number of infections in the days following a protest'), but they were prepared to accept this because they believed in the BLM cause.

The irony of public-health professionals encouraging large crowds to assemble in the middle of a pandemic was not lost on everyone who participated. Catherine Troisi, an epidemiologist at the University of Texas Health Science Center, told the *New York Times*: 'I certainly condemned the anti-lockdown protests at the time, and I'm not condemning the protests now, and I struggle with that. I have a hard time articulating why that is okay.'

Similarly, Mark Lurie, professor of epidemiology at Brown University, said 'we have to be honest: a few weeks before, we were criticising protesters for arguing to open up the economy and saying that was dangerous behaviour. I am still grappling with that.'

The hypocrisy was so glaring that even the *Guardian* noticed it. In an article titled, 'We often accuse the right of distorting science. But the left changed the coronavirus narrative overnight', Thomas Chatterton Williams wrote: 'Two weeks ago we shamed people for being in the street; today we shame them for not being in the street ... The climate-change-denying right is often ridiculed, correctly, for politicising science. Yet the way the public-health narrative around coronavirus has reversed itself overnight seems an awful lot like ... politicising science.'

A month later, on the other side of the ocean, Public Health England found itself in the news for two reasons. On 17 July, health secretary Matt Hancock announced an urgent enquiry into its miscounting of Covid-19 deaths. It had been revealed that PHE had been counting the death of anybody who had ever tested positive for the coronavirus as a Covid-19 fatality, thereby exaggerating the death toll. It was the latest in a long list of failures from PHE that would soon lead to it being scrapped. On the same day, as if to remind everyone of where PHE had been focusing its efforts, it was announced that a number of chocolate bars, including Wispa and Twirl, would be reduced in size as part of PHE's sugar-reduction scheme to ensure they complied with the agency's calorie cap for confectionery.

These small tales tell a bigger story about the absurdity and irrelevance of the modern 'public health' movement. Covid-19 has exposed the gaps between what people think 'public health' does, what people in 'public health' think they do, and what they actually do. The public thinks their job is to protect us from infectious disease.

'Public health' professionals think their job is to 'speak truth to power' and tackle racism, poverty and inequality. What they actually do is make minor adjustments to chocolate bars.

The BLM letter perfectly illustrated the tension between what people think the 'public health' profession does (protect them from infectious diseases and environmental hazards) and what people who work in 'public health' want to do (political campaigning and virtue-signalling). When forced to choose between these conflicting objectives, political campaigning won out. 'Public health' professionals effectively sided with the virus.

They normally don't have to make such an awkward choice. In the absence of infectious disease, the 'public health' establishment has spent 40 years incorporating all the bogeymen of dull-witted progressives – consumerism, capitalism, Americanism, individualism, etc – into an overarching narrative about 'health inequalities' and the 'social determinants of health', which allows them to campaign for restrictions on freedom, higher taxes, a bigger state and more funding for themselves.

Insofar as the public was aware that this was going on, it was done on the tacit understanding that the 'public health' establishment would be there for us if a genuine public-health crisis occurred. Covid-19 pulled the rug from under that illusion. When the pandemic emerged, Public Health England went to pieces. Its CEO was nowhere to be seen. Local public-health directors became headless chickens. PHE failed to increase testing capacity sufficiently. It virtually ceased community testing just as the virus was getting in its stride. It not only opposed the use of face masks, but also actively encouraged the Advertising Standards Authority to ban adverts for them. In the end, it couldn't even make a sensible estimate of how many people had died from the virus.

There was a palpable sense of relief at PHE when obesity was fingered as a risk factor for Covid-19, because it allowed the agency to retreat into its comfort zone of lifestyle regulation. Finally! An aspect of the problem that could be superficially addressed with an advertising ban! If only those Twirls had been made slightly smaller a few years earlier!

PHE is now on the scrapheap and will be replaced by a facsimile of the Health Protection Agency, which focused solely on genuine public-health issues and was itself replaced by PHE in 2013. The implosion of PHE when tested by a genuine public-health crisis seems like a 'You Had One Job' moment, but the whole problem was that it didn't have one job, at least not as far as the people running it were concerned. From the outset, PHE officially stated that its 'primary duty is to protect the public from infectious diseases and other environmental hazards', but when Duncan Selbie became its first (and last) CEO in 2013, the *Lancet* reported that 'he firmly believes that the key factors to good health lie in tackling the underlying social determinants: "Jobs, homes, and friends are what will make the biggest difference to improving people's health."'

This may be true, but providing jobs, homes and friends was beyond his remit. Reasonable people disagree on the best way to secure jobs and homes. This is why they are political issues, not public-health issues. And even the biggest fan of government intervention would admit that the state cannot force people to be your friend.

Similarly, the World Health Organisation long ago moved beyond the tedious business of tackling infectious disease and began prioritising issues such as gender equality, poverty reduction and universal healthcare. Again, these are laudable aims, but the people at the WHO have no particular expertise outside of medicine, no legislative power, and no obvious means by which they can achieve any of these aims.

We could tolerate 'public health' professionals banging on about complex socio-economic problems beyond their ken if they could do their day job. Covid-19 showed that they can't. The WHO was a hapless dupe of the Chinese Communist Party in the crucial early stages, while Public Health England was just hapless. Like the broader 'public health' movement, these agencies had taken their eye off infectious diseases in favour of becoming glorified political campaigners. Endless conferences, studies, targets and position statements on everything from computer games to climate change were no use when push came to shove.

This is how 'public health' lost its way. Almost anything can be linked to physical or mental health, but that does not make them public-health issues. And even if we arbitrarily redefined racism or inequality or gambling or whatever as public-health issues, it wouldn't make those who work in 'public health' better able to tackle them than the average concerned citizen. For all the blather about the 'social determinants of health', the only tangible policies that have emerged from 'public health' involve hassling people about what they eat, drink and smoke.

The most polite way of putting it is that the 'public health' movement has spread itself too thinly over too many issues. Put less politely, the modern 'public health' establishment is, at best, a waste of space. At worst, it is a menace. From local councils to the World Health Organisation, it is a parade of midwits who are unable to do the things they want to do, incapable of doing the things they should be doing, and shouldn't be doing the things they do.

4 SEPTEMBER 2020

EXTINCTION REBELLION: RADICAL REACTIONARIES

PADDY HANNAM

Green protest group Extinction Rebellion has been described as far left and even Marxist by some of its critics. For opponents from the right, XR is a revolutionary movement hoping to upend the modern world. Some suggest the more radical end of environmentalism is not really about climate change at all, but rather is a vehicle for a broader political vision.

No doubt, many of these so-called rebels believe they are, in fact, part of a revolutionary project that is changing society for the better. In the UK, we've all seen their weird banners, bizarre costumes, poorly thought-out stunts and huge demands. Some surely do see themselves as left-wing radicals. Certainly, some have unorthodox ideas. But Marxists? I'm not so sure.

Let's look at what they want. For all the attention XR types give to the UK and other Western nations, their project would essentially necessitate the perpetual impoverishment of the world's poor – which is hardly a left-wing or Marxist aim. While XR focuses its actions on the policies of Western states, hundreds of millions, if not billions, of people would have their lives and livelihoods worsened by such transformations as the abandonment of fossil fuels.

Take poverty as an example. Enormous progress has been made in this area in recent decades. In the 25 years up to 2018, over a billion people came out of absolute poverty – a number greater than the entire population still living in absolute poverty today. Between 2013 and 2015 alone, the number of people living on less than $1.90 per day fell by 68million.

This progress is truly remarkable. Though it has not been clearly noticeable in the West, it is in many ways the result of a re-enactment of Europe's industrial revolutions of the 19th century in other parts of the world. In this sense, it has given new life to the words of

Karl Marx, who said the following about the transformation of
the UK from a feudal society into a modern capitalist economy:

> 'It is the working millions of Great Britain who first have laid down –
> the real basis of a new society – modern industry, which transformed
> the destructive agencies of nature into the productive power of man.
> The English working classes, with invincible energies, by the sweat
> of their brows and brains, have called into life the material means of
> ennobling labour itself, and of multiplying its fruits to such a degree
> as to make general abundance possible.'

In other words, the advent of capitalism heralded the newfound
ability of mankind to harness the power of the natural world to its
ends – to conquer nature. In achieving this, the working masses of
newly industrial economies like Britain's did something spectacular:
they made possible mass lifestyle changes that, just a century earlier,
could have been only dreamed of. For the first time, society's poorest
were freed from dependence on the seasons and feudal masters for
their supply of food and for their freedom.

For Marx, this was *good*, at least in comparison with what went
before. He waxed lyrical about the incredible and unprecedented
productive power of capitalism because it had facilitated the
transformation of the world for the better:

> 'The bourgeoisie, during its rule of scarce one hundred years, has
> created more massive and more colossal productive forces than have
> all preceding generations together. Subjection of Nature's forces to
> man, machinery, application of chemistry to industry and agriculture,
> steam-navigation, railways, electric telegraphs, clearing of whole
> continents for cultivation, canalisation of rivers, whole populations
> conjured out of the ground – what earlier century had even a
> presentiment that such productive forces slumbered in the lap
> of social labour?'

Obviously, this progress came at a cost. Marx is better known for his
condemnation of capitalism as a morally unjust system, which tears
apart families and alienates people from their work and from each
other, than he is for his acknowledgement that it is an improvement
on feudalism. But noting this acknowledgement is essential to any
comprehensive understanding of what Marx thought.

Now contrast this with the sometimes neo-feudalistic campaigns of modern environmentalists, many of whom want us to abandon the kind of production that made the modern world.

Consider their anti-human demands for a huge reduction in the global population. This would represent mankind's retreat from dominance over nature, a position for which it has fought for all time. Rather than seeing 'populations conjured out of the ground', as before, we would see the walls closing in on humanity.

Or think of those who responded to the Covid-induced collapse in the use of transport, the closure of energy-consuming businesses, and the reappearance of wild animals in newly quiet towns, by saying it all proved that we could, in fact, achieve the aim of a green world. After all, all it required was the destruction of the economy, an assault on civil liberties, and the deaths of hundreds of thousands of people. Not to mention the descent of vast numbers into extreme poverty.

Greta Thunberg has condemned Western leaders' 'fairytales of eternal economic growth'. But economic growth benefits everyone, not just the rich. In fact, it is far more important for the worst-off that economies grow — without that advancement, they have little hope of escaping poverty.

The truth is that modern environmentalism's key demands are mutually exclusive with keeping up the kind of human progress we have seen in recent decades. The globe cannot afford immediately and completely to ditch fossil fuels. More precisely, its poorest inhabitants cannot afford to. It is they who will most sharply feel the consequences of the often gas-filled pipeline of economic growth being turned off. Middle-class activists in rich Western countries, in contrast, will cope.

Extinction Rebellion and its ilk want us to turn back the clock. They seek not a new world but a kind of new feudal order. They want mankind to retire from innovation and advancement and shrink in number. In the name of freedom, progress and the advancement of the prospects of the world's poorest, leftists should oppose them.

Marx wrote that, 'The labouring classes have conquered nature'. The next step for him was not to let nature take back control, as eco-activists of today desire — it was for the workers to 'conquer man'.

10 SEPTEMBER 2020

WHO RULES?

MICK HUME

Does the UK government's Internal Market Bill threaten to break international law, even if only, as one gormless minister claimed, in a 'limited and specific way'? That is the question being endlessly batted back and forth between Boris Johnson's supporters and critics.

Let us leave that mind-numbing debate to the constitutional lawyers for now. Because for the rest of us, it's surely the wrong question to ask. The real issue in the inflated row over the Internal Market Bill, as in everything to do with Brexit, is: who rules?

Brexit is a power struggle, not an exercise in legal semantics. Do we truly live in a democratic nation state, where power rests with accountable rulers who we elect – and can get rid of? Or are we to be subject to the power of unelected EU officials, commissioners and judges (imposed with the support of the UK establishment)?

The demand for more sovereignty and democracy was the decisive driver behind the revolt of 17.4million Leave voters in the EU referendum. On the other side of this struggle, the Remainer elites (not to be confused with all of the 16.1million who voted Remain) want to keep real power as far removed as possible from the demos – the people.

That is why they have fought tooth and nail for more than four years to derail a real Brexit. And it is why arch Remainers from all parties, such as former prime ministers Tony Blair and John Major, are outraged by the Internal Market Bill, which could give the UK government power to override aspects of the EU Withdrawal Agreement.

The Remainer elites insist upon 'upholding international law' because they see it as a counter to *national* law, made by our elected national parliament. Their ideal of international law is a power above and beyond the grasp of voters. That's why they now talk about it as if it were a secular form of God's law, handed down from a mountain on stone tablets, rather than cooked up by diplomats in secret, smoke-free rooms and enforced by unaccountable judges.

This Remainer vision of international law captures the essence of the European Union. The EU is a self-avowedly 'supranational' system, whose powers reside over and above any national parliament, in the hands of commissioners, committees and judges. When elected governments join the European Council, they cease to act as nation states and instead become 'member states', accountable to the EU behind closed doors rather than to their own electorates.

In 1991, leading left-wing Labour MP Tony Benn made a famous speech in the House of Commons defending parliamentary democracy and opposing the Maastricht Treaty, which would create the ever-more federal European Union of today. This, Benn rightly insisted, would mean members of parliament handing their powers over to unelected bodies, using the instrument of 'the Royal Prerogative of treaty-making'. It would leave the British people as powerless and unrepresented as they had been under absolute monarchy, before the historic struggle for democracy succeeded. Thirty years later, many who claim Benn's mantle on the Labour left seemingly want to uphold 'the Royal Prerogative of treaty-making' over the rights of parliamentary democracy.

National sovereignty is the precondition for democracy, since the nation state is still the only basis on which democratic systems work. Any talk of 'Europe-wide democracy' or 'global democracy' simply means in practice the rule of bodies such as the EU Commission and the UN Security Council. If we are to live in a democracy, national parliaments that are elected by and accountable to their peoples must have the power to make national law – and to seek to amend or override any other.

Indeed, the modern concept of international law itself was arguably founded as a recognition of the primacy of national sovereignty. In 1648 the international treaties that ended the 30 Years' War established the system known as 'Westphalian

Sovereignty'. This proto-international law recognised for the first time the concepts of the inviolability of national borders, and non-interference in the domestic affairs of sovereign states. It meant that supranational powers such as the Holy Roman Empire should not have the right to dictate to sovereign nations.

If that was deemed important in the 17th century, when Europe was still ruled by princes and the first stirrings of modern democracy were just emerging in the English Revolution, how much more important national sovereignty ought to be now that we live in national democracies. Instead, international law has often been turned into an instrument of today's global elites, who wish to degrade and even demonise national sovereignty and democracy. That is why they are up in arms about the UK government's rare moment of resistance through the Internal Market Bill.

Of course, Conservative prime minister Johnson made a rod for his own back by endorsing the disastrous Withdrawal Agreement last year – the sort of surrender treaty that, as many of us pointed out at the time, is usually signed only after losing a war. However, under pressure from Brexiteers, Boris eventually contested and won the December 2019 General Election on a manifesto that effectively repudiated parts of the Withdrawal Agreement and pledged that the UK would not be tied to EU rules. Now he appears to be trying to get out of the mess he helped to make in order to keep his promise to the electorate.

In this, the government is not 'breaking the law'. It is making the law, by proposing a bill and getting it voted through parliament. That is what governments are elected to do in a democracy. To try to insist that 'international law' somehow supersedes the process of democratic politics looks like the latest bad case of what some of us used to call legal cretinism.

Those who now insist on the primacy of international law are essentially saying that our national system of law-making has too much democracy. In fact, our system of parliamentary representation is not nearly democratic enough. We saw that through the years after 2016 when a Remainer-dominated parliament sought to thwart the will of millions of Leave voters. We can see it now as Remainers, having lost at the polls, seek once more to use the House of Lords, the most anti-democratic assembly in the Western world, to kill the bill. Brexit is only the beginning of the battle to take control.

As the question of 'who rules?' returns to the top of the political agenda, let us remind them all of the original meaning of democracy: the meeting of the *demos* — Ancient Greek for the people — with *kratos*, meaning power and control. There is no room for u-turns in the battle for Brexit and democracy.

17 SEPTEMBER 2020

WHY THEY HATE SWEDEN

FRASER MYERS

Before the coronavirus, Sweden for most people symbolised moderation and fairness. But since the pandemic hit, this Scandinavian social democracy has been maligned like few other countries on Earth. The reason is, of course, that Sweden did not follow the rest of the world into lockdown. And because even their proponents recognise that lockdowns come at an extraordinarily high price – eviscerating our freedoms, laying waste to our economies and even damaging our health – the only European country that attempted to tread a more liberal path became the target of an extreme and hysterical smear campaign.

Throughout the spring and early summer, the negative headlines were relentless. The *New York Times* repeatedly branded Sweden a 'pariah state'; its no-lockdown policy apparently made it the 'world's cautionary tale'.

The liberal *Guardian* used to regularly hail Sweden as a model to emulate, one which 'right-wingers' were 'desperate' to see fail. But during the pandemic, the same paper denounced Sweden as a 'model for the right' and branded its Covid policy a 'deadly folly'.

According to this view, Sweden's policy was not only misguided but also sinister. The refusal to shut down society was akin to playing 'Russian roulette' with people's lives. Public support in Sweden for the less restrictive policy revealed 'the dark side of nationalism', which could pose a danger to 'vulnerable minorities', according to the *Washington Post*.

The world looked on in fascination and terror as Swedes were still allowed to go to bars and restaurants, schools remained open for everyone under 16, and gatherings were still permitted for up to 50 people. For Anders Tegnell, the man in charge of Sweden's Covid policy, full-on lockdown was 'using a hammer to kill a fly'.

The media consensus was that Sweden was conducting a dangerous 'experiment' in 'Swedo-science', which had 'well and truly failed'. But in reality, it was the rest of the world that was playing a cruel experiment, which disrupted people's lives for little gain.

As we entered the autumn, the UK, France, Spain and other European countries were panicking over rising Covid case numbers, and the contrast with Sweden's situation became harder to ignore. *The Times* told us that 'Sweden's low positive test rate "vindicates [its] coronavirus strategy"'. The *Sun* pointed out that 'lockdown-free Sweden' had recorded its 'lowest number of Covid cases since March', as 'other countries' were hit by a 'second wave'. And the *Guardian* acknowledged that Sweden was spared the 'European surge as coronavirus infections stay low'.

Even the *Financial Times*, which has been at the forefront of Britain's lockdown lobby, was forced to report the good news about Sweden. It even carried an approving interview with the now world-(in)famous Tegnell.

Governments and health officials have started paying attention, too (though clearly not enough). In September, Sweden became one of the few countries on the UK's travel corridor, meaning that arrivals from Sweden no longer had to quarantine — unlike arrivals from Spain and France, which applied stringent lockdowns. Johan Giesecke, a strident critic of lockdown who played a key role in advising the Swedish health authorities, has been awarded a promotion at the World Health Organisation to advise on all things pandemic-related.

Sweden's critics like to compare its Covid death rate with its Scandinavian neighbours. But back in May, health chiefs in Norway discovered that the so-called R-number (the rate at which the virus spreads) had already fallen to 1.1 *before* its lockdown was put in place. This led the head of Norway's public-health agency to conclude that 'we could possibly have achieved the same effects and avoided some of the unfortunate impacts by not locking down, but by instead keeping open but with infection-control measures' — a tacit approval of the Swedish strategy.

In Denmark, public-health experts have tried to distance themselves from the government's lockdown policy. They claim that the Danish prime minister 'abused healthcare advice' when she said 'the authorities' recommended lockdown. This was taken by most of the public to mean the Danish Health Authority and the infectious-diseases agency. In fact, the Danish Health Authority had recommended very few of the draconian measures that were eventually implemented.

Lockdown advocates relished Sweden's apparently high death rate. So far it has been higher than many European countries, but lower than some others that pursued strict lockdowns. (Belgium has had both the strictest lockdown and highest death rate in Europe, and, globally, Peru looks set to pull off the same catastrophic feat.) Modelling for Sweden predicted deaths in the tens of thousands, but this never materialised.

The Swedophobes also delighted in tales of Sweden's economic woes. 'They literally gained nothing', gloated one expert in the *New York Times*: 'It's a self-inflicted wound, and they have no economic gains.' At the time, Sweden's economy was faring almost as badly as everywhere else in Europe. But it has since become clear it was hit much less hard than other major countries. In August, the Swedish government pulled off the astonishing feat of generating a budget surplus.

When countries followed each other into lockdown, Anders Tegnell remarked that it was 'as if the world had gone mad'. Though much of the world seemed to believe he was the lunatic in charge of the asylum, history may well look upon Sweden very differently.

21 SEPTEMBER 2020

THE PROBLEM WITH THE SUPREME COURT

LUKE GITTOS

US Supreme Court justice Ruth Bader Ginsburg has died. She was
87 years old.

Ginsburg reportedly dictated a dying wish to her granddaughter,
which read 'my most fervent wish is that I will not be replaced until
a new president is installed'. Nevertheless, President Donald Trump
and Senate majority leader Mitch McConnell vowed to press on
with nominating a new justice before the US election.

Ginsburg famously refused to stand down while Barack Obama
was president, despite going through surgery for cancer in 2009.
Some have argued that it was her veneration by sections of the left
that kept her going. In 2013, she had a Tumblr account devoted to her,
which gave her the name 'Notorious RBG'. A Netflix documentary
about her career presented her as a trailblazing champion of equality.

This was hardly undeserved. Ginsburg argued significant cases
before the court in advance of gender equality during the 1970s.
She was lukewarm in support of reproductive freedom in her earlier
judgements, but in later life she was a vocal supporter of a woman's
right to choose. Some commentators have highlighted how the
American pro-choice movement has a fight on its hands following
Ginsburg's death, with some anticipating an attack on *Roe v Wade*.

Democratic leaders have suggested they could run the election
on a platform of 'structural court reforms'. Some have interpreted
this to mean that a Democratic Congress would 'pack the court',
by changing the number of justices to increase the number of
progressive justices. Former presidential candidate Pete Buttigieg
has suggested that the court should consist of five Democrats,
five Republicans and five 'apolitical' justices, in order to counter the
effect of a conservative majority. To achieve this, Democrats would

need to regain control over both Congress and the White House.

But it is not Ginsburg's death that poses a threat to progressive values in the US. Nor is it the current constitution of the court or the number of justices. It is the reliance that activists have come to place on the Supreme Court as their chosen vehicle for pushing change. These proposed reforms show how dependent the American left has become on *litigating* for radical change, rather than arguing for it on the streets and in public.

Historically, the US Supreme Court has often held back progressive social change – even in the face of democratic pressure. Frederick Douglass once remarked that slavery could not be defeated by relying on anti-slavery jurisprudence in the Supreme Court, but instead through 'the court of common sense and common humanity'. The historian Howard Zinn has described how the court failed even to hear a case by US soldiers who refused to fight in Vietnam, on the basis that there had been no formal declaration of war by Congress. Nor did the court enforce the First Amendment when Congress made it illegal to criticise the First World War. As Zinn says, 'those rights only come alive when citizens organise, protest, demonstrate, strike, boycott, rebel and violate the law in order to uphold justice'.

The position that the court holds in American democracy is well illustrated by the discussion around voting rights. One of Ginsburg's famous dissents was in the case of *Shelby County v Holder*. The decision invalidated a 'coverage formula' that meant certain jurisdictions had to seek 'pre-clearance' from the federal government before passing new voting laws. In the aftermath of the decision, new voter-identification laws have passed in many states, making it harder for certain people to vote. Some commentators have described the decision of the court as 'setting a new era of white hegemony'. Voting laws can lead to democratic outrages, such as voters being denied a vote on the basis of minor debts to the state. But these are democratic problems that have to be resolved by state legislatures. Attempting to fix problems with democracy through the law has always been a fool's errand. The character of the court is fundamentally conservative and it has often come up short in defending fundamental rights.

Philosopher Alexis de Tocqueville remarked that 'a more imposing judicial power was never constituted by any people' than the US Supreme Court. Ginsburg's death highlights how the court still holds too much power over American democracy. Progressives in America should not attempt to neutralise a Trump appointment through changes to the court's composition. They should argue for restricting the court's power and increasing the power of the legislature. The power of popular movements can be far more consequential than the decisions of the Supreme Court. This is a lesson from history that American progressives seem unwilling to learn.

22 SEPTEMBER 2020

HOW ACTIVISM BECAME SKIN-DEEP

ELLA WHELAN

Super tweeter and actress Jameela Jamil worked her way back on to Twitter's trending list recently after getting into a spat with someone about skincare.

When a fan praised Jamil's blemish-free face after she posted a classic, make-up-free 'look how naturally beautiful I am' selfie on Instagram, Jamil launched into a lecture on how 'privileged people have more access to good quality nutrition and also our lives are significantly less stressful than the lives of those with less privilege'. After being mocked for her inability to take a compliment, Jamil managed to wring out yet more 'controversy' over her comments in not one, not two, not three, but four further posts to fans.

Jamil is no stranger to tiresome Twitterspats. Most notable was when a journalist accused her of having Munchausen's syndrome. Over the years, Jamil has claimed to have been attacked by killer bees at least three times and to have been involved in two car accidents (the first, she says, resulted in her needing a Zimmer frame, the second a wheelchair). She also claims to have survived multiple cancer scares and seems to have varying degrees of peanut tolerance, depending on the day.

Aside from her day job as an actress on NBC's *The Good Place*, Jamil seems to have dedicated her life to being an 'activist', showing how degraded that word has become. One of her outlets is a group called the I Weigh Community, which was originally set up as an Instagram account. It seeks to pursue 'radical inclusivity' and to 'mobilise activism'. While the account has of late branched out into political issues, from climate change to trans rights, it was originally dedicated to campaigning against diet pills and 'skinny privilege', while teaching women to realise that we are more than what we weigh.

This kind of pop 'activism' centres on a narcissistic obsession with privilege, self-worth and so-called self-care that would have made Christopher Lasch's head spin. But it's just one example of how self-centred much of contemporary politics has become — especially quasi-feminist campaigns that claim to be 'empowering' women.

Instagram and other social-media platforms populated by young, impressionable girls are often said to be bad for mental health, as they're filled with unrealistic beauty standards and sexist representations of women. But the best way to gain social capital on social media these days is not to flaunt your perfections on the outside, but to fetishise your imperfections on the inside. It's no longer cool to post sexy pictures. Instead, you should show off your mental-health challenges, your anxiety, your fears and your self-loathing. If you're as good-looking as Jamil, a bit of both won't hurt.

This framing of politics through our inner lives — which seems to be far more pronounced among women — is deeply damaging. What it suggests is that life has to mould around our insecurities and sense of self, rather than us being rough, tough and strong enough to adapt to or challenge the world around us. This form of feminist politics has, in many ways, given up on changing the outside world. Instead it encourages women to prioritise introspection as a means of achieving political fulfilment.

This has encouraged an almost Victorian understanding of women as constantly needing to have our honour protected and our sensibilities cosseted. The sexist view of women as weaker and less able than men has been reheated and served up in social-media posts about Safe Spaces, checking your privilege and using the correct language.

We might laugh at the lunacy of Jamil and her contemporaries. But we should be concerned about the way today's identity politics prioritises victimhood over strength, protection over freedom, and the self over engagement with society. This is a serious threat to those of us who want to change the world, rather than bicker about the privilege of skincare.

24 SEPTEMBER 2020

THE BATTLE FOR AMERICA'S SOUL

FRANK FUREDI

The attitude of Western cultural and political establishments towards the past has changed dramatically. They no longer view it as a source of pride or present-day inspiration. Rather, they view it as a source of shame and even guilt. The 'good old days', it seems, are no more.

It is the narrative of 'the bad old days' that is culturally dominant now. Warnings highlighting 'outdated attitudes' accompany reruns of old films and TV shows. Museums present their exhibits as sources of colonial shame. And schools encourage young people to be ashamed of their ancestors. Everywhere one looks, history appears as little more than a toxic tale of racism, misogyny and abuse.

There has been very little opposition to this narrative of the bad old days, and this has only encouraged its elitist, identitarian advocates. So much so, in fact, that they are now using this war against the past to discredit their present-day opponents. And no one is doing so with more sophistication than the *New York Times* and its '1619 Project'.

In the mainstream media, Trump is often accused of starting a culture war, or of using history to portray himself as a 'defender of American heritage'. Unsurprisingly, this happened again when Trump took the opportunity of a 'White House Conference on American History' to announce he was setting up a '1776 Commission', to 'defend the legacy of America's founding'.

What Trump's detractors overlook is that it was not him who started this current phase of the culture wars. That honour falls to the 1619 Project, which was launched by the *Times* in 2019.

By the time Trump delivered his speech, more than a year later, the 1619 Project had won the support of most of America's cultural elite, from Hollywood to universities, and Nikole Hannah-Jones, its lead author, had been awarded the prestigious Pulitzer Prize.

So Trump was not starting anything with his plan for a 1776 Commission. He was responding to the increasing momentum of the 1619 Project and its role in today's political unrest. He sensed that it was no longer just history at stake; it was the soul of the nation, too.

As the 1619 Project's title suggests, it claims that the year 1619, and not 1776, is the true founding year of the US. This, it argues, is because the US was effectively founded for the purpose of entrenching slavery, in 1619, the year African slaves first arrived in Jamestown. The actual founding of the US in the American Revolution is dismissed as a selfish attempt to preserve the exploitative and oppressive legacy of 1619. And the Declaration of Independence and the US's then remarkably advanced liberal and democratic constitution are implicitly renounced as slave-owners' charters.

In this way, the 1619 Project is a self-conscious attempt to contaminate and undermine the very foundation on which the American way of life has been built. It is therefore a profound political attack on the present. Indeed, Hannah-Jones herself admits that its principal objective is not to shed new light on the past, but to undermine the moral authority of the present. 'I've always said that the 1619 Project is not a history', she writes. 'It is a work of journalism that explicitly seeks to challenge the national narrative and, therefore, national memory. The project has always been as much about the present as it is about the past.'

So this is a project devoted to the toxification of the past in order to delegitimise the present-day institutions of the US. In doing so, the 1619 Project erases the boundary not just between the present and the past, but also between truth and fiction. In 1619, the African slaves, like many white people sent to Virginia, became indentured labourers, not slaves. This is not a nitpicking distinction. It shows that it is wholly inaccurate to claim that the US was founded to entrench slavery. Other eminent historians have also drawn attention to the numerous liberties the 1619 Project has taken with the facts. Such has been the level of historical criticism levelled at the project that the *Times* edited out its claim that 1619 was the 'true founding' of America. Hannah-Jones went so far as to deny, on CNN, that she had ever intended to replace 1776 with the new founding date of 1619. The project's casual approach to historical fact shows just how politicised and cynical the whole enterprise is.

Trump himself took issue with the project's attempt to portray America's foundation as being based on 'oppression, not freedom'. He countered, saying that the Declaration of Independence 'set in motion the unstoppable chain of events that abolished slavery, secured civil rights, defeated Communism and fascism, and built the most fair, equal, and prosperous nation in human history'.

The aim of Trump's 1776 Commission is to counterbalance the gloomy take on America's past now taught in American schools. 'We must clear away the twisted web of lies in our schools and classrooms', he said, 'and teach our children the magnificent truth about our country'.

But it is unlikely that, by itself, the 1776 Commission can match the cultural power of its opponents. After all, the educational establishment is extremely hostile to the teaching of what sounds like patriotic history. 'It's disgusting', was the predictable reaction of Randi Weingarten, president of the American Federation of Teachers, to Trump's speech. Others said Trump's version of the founding 'revolv[ed] around white males'. For educators brought up on a diet of identity politics, denouncing dead white males is something of a quasi-religious duty.

Still, although it was only one speech promising a single commission, Trump's comments do represent an overdue attempt to join the battle for America's soul. Virtually every issue raised in the course of the current phase of the culture wars is ultimately linked to the perceived authority of the foundation of America.

The Latin term *auctoritas* refers to foundational authority. Foundational authority provides certain political decisions or opinions with a source of legitimacy. Throughout much of modern history it is the absence of precisely this foundational authority that has haunted public life. Political instability and institutional fragility are symptoms of societies that lack an authoritative foundation on which to draw.

The founding of the US, and its articulation in the Declaration of Independence and the Constitution, is arguably the most successful example of the act of foundation in the modern era. Political philosopher Hannah Arendt regarded it as a unique event not just for Americans, but also for humanity as a whole. In her essay, 'Founding Fathers', she wrote that the challenge of realising freedom demanded a 'new foundation', a demonstration that humanity 'can begin something altogether new'. Arendt observed that:

> '[T]he question of the foundation of a republic was how to preserve this spirit, the revolutionary spirit, how to find lasting institutions which could prevent this experience from being the experience of only one generation.'

The preservation of the spirit of foundation was successfully realised in the Constitution of the United States.

As Arendt explained, the difference between the US Constitution and those of postwar Europe, 'which were given from above, usually by experts', is that only in America was the Constitution 'an event', an act of foundation. And, almost uniquely, the US Constitution has been revered ever since. As she remarked:

> 'One is tempted to conclude that the remembrance of the event itself – a people deliberately founding a new body politic dedicated to freedom – has shrouded the document in an atmosphere of reverent awe and shielded it against the onslaught of time and circumstances.'

She concluded on an optimistic note:

> 'One also is tempted to predict that the authority of the republic will be safe as long as the act itself, the beginning as such, is remembered as the promise it holds out, and was meant to hold out, for all those who, by virtue of birth, enter earthly life as beginners.'

Arendt wrote 'Founding Fathers' in 1963. At that point in time, her optimism about the future of the republic was justified, because the normative underpinning of the US's foundation was rarely questioned. Those who questioned the dark moments of

American history — such as the practice of slavery, or certain racist policies — did so on the grounds that they violated the norms of freedom and equality enshrined in the Constitution. The Constitution was therefore seen as a corrective to, say, racial oppression, not as its embodiment.

Today, however, the promise of America's foundation is under constant attack. Too many in the US are losing touch with the idealism and the spirit of freedom and democracy that inspired the founding of a new world. That is why, contrary to Arendt, the republic is no longer safe. The toxification of the act of America's foundation by cultural and educational elites, and self-styled radicals, writ large in the 1619 Project, is corroding the legitimacy of America's constitution and institutions. The decay of the republic, the detachment of its present from its often inspiring past, will not only affect the people of America. For America's founding is also a central part of the intellectual and moral legacy of all of humanity. That is why those of us watching events in America from afar have every reason to join the battle for its soul.

28 SEPTEMBER 2020

THE NEW RACISM

FRASER MYERS

There is something unsavoury about the new 'anti-racism' —
sometimes referred to as critical race theory or racial identity
politics. Something, well, a bit racist. It is therefore not remotely
surprising that infamous 'white nationalist' Richard Spencer has
been able to find common ground with one of America's most
celebrated anti-racist activists, Ibram X Kendi.

Kendi, born Ibram Henry Rogers, is the author of *How To Be
An Antiracist*, which rocketed back up the bestseller list during
the summer of Black Lives Matter. His basic thesis is that everything
can be divided into two categories: racist and anti-racist. There is,
he argues, no such thing as 'not racist', because 'not racist' means
being neutral in the struggle against racism. It is merely, therefore,
'a mask for racism'.

So then what should we make of Kendi's recent bizarre tirade
against interracial adoption? Is it racist or anti-racist? Responding
to a picture of President Trump's Supreme Court pick, Amy Coney
Barrett, with her adopted black children from Haiti, Kendi tweeted:
'Some white colonisers "adopted" black children. They "civilised"
these "savage" children in the "superior" ways of white people, while
using them as props in their lifelong pictures of denial, while cutting
the biological parents of these children out of the picture of humanity.'
The language he employs sounds anti-racist — condemning a
real historical ill. But the conclusion one surely has to draw from
his reasoning is racist. How could anyone support this continued
'colonisation' of black children?

It turns out that white supremacists share a similar disgust with
interracial adoption. 'Not wrong', concurred Richard Spencer on
Twitter. Yes, that is the same Richard Spencer who calls for the

ethnic cleansing of America and the reconstitution of the European Union as a white racial empire.

Of course, Kendi is wrong. Barrett is not a coloniser but an adoptive parent in 21st-century America. Mixed-race families are now so common as to be mundane. Yet Kendi's rage is illustrative of how even something so innocent is now viewed by those who claim to be 'anti-racist' with suspicion and hostility. Segregationists infamously held up obscene placards declaring that 'race mixing is communism' – perhaps Kendi and his ilk believe 'race mixing is colonialism'.

Kendi insists that his comments were taken out of context by 'bots', and he says he does not believe that white parents of black children are 'inherently' racist. But if we were to be charitable and say that Kendi is merely being misinterpreted, he is also being misinterpreted by his woke fans.

Back in July, a white New York City education councillor provoked deafening screams of outrage for the perfectly innocent activity of bouncing a black baby on his knee (the baby was his friend's nephew). 'It hurts people when they see a white man bouncing a brown baby on their lap', a fellow councillor screamed in indignation over a Zoom chat. 'That is harmful. That makes people cry. It makes people log out of our meeting.' She then reveals where this rage comes from: 'Read a book! Read Ibram Kendi!' Whether intentional or not, 'interracial interactions are bad' seems to be the takeaway message from one of America's bestselling anti-racist authors.

The logic of segregation lurks beneath so much of what passes as anti-racism today. If a white person were to announce that they believed the hallmarks of 'whiteness' are 'politeness', 'hard work' and 'objective, rational thinking', you might suspect they were an old-school white chauvinist. But this list of supposedly 'white' traits actually comes from the Smithsonian's National Museum of African American History and Culture (NMAAHC), as part of a collection of Black Lives Matter-inspired teaching materials. The implication is that black and white people hold different, alien, perhaps even unbridgeable values.

These 'anti-racist' ideas now manifest themselves in racially segregated spaces. Consider the short-lived experiment of the 'Capitol Hill Autonomous Zone' (CHAZ), which sprung up in Seattle after the George Floyd protests. Some of the protesters set up a 'Blackout' area in a field — a segregated, black-only 'healing space', which was, ironically, guarded by mainly white activists. Many US universities now offer racially segregated commencement events. Such segregation is, of course, not driven by the same impulses as Jim Crow or the ones that motivate the likes of Richard Spencer. Instead, it is justified on the belief that people of colour are perpetual victims, and white people are perpetual oppressors.

What racists and today's 'anti-racists' share in common above all is a belief in the significance of race. They see race as a defining feature of one's character, one's values and one's place in the world. And that is why both sets of ideas produce outcomes, attitudes and policies that are so obviously racist. We need to reject racial thinking in all its forms and instead aim to transcend race entirely.

30 SEPTEMBER 2020

AND A PLAGUE SHALL COVER THE LAND OF TRUMP

BRENDAN O'NEILL

This is a moment that 'feels Biblical', says Maureen Dowd at the *New York Times*. She is talking, of course, about President Trump being struck down by the plague, by Covid. Going full Leviticus, Dowd marvels at the karmic retribution of this chief doubter of Covid now being infected by Covid, of this blasphemer against experts now suffering the fate that experts warned would befall him if he didn't comply with their rituals of mask-wearing and lockdowns. 'The implacable virus has come to his door', Dowd writes, giving Covid-19 sentience, power almost: the power to smite its unbelievers. *Implacable*: that means something that cannot be appeased. That's Covid, apparently: the insatiable beast, the terrible god, who will brook no questioning.

Dowd isn't the only Trump-basher getting all Biblical over Covid's visitation upon the White House. Across the commentariat and the Twittersphere there is much *Schadenfreude* that the man who scoffed at the idea that he should change his entire life in response to a virus must now meekly, weakly watch as the virus has 'come to his door'. 'It's hard to overlook the symbolism of Trump's positive test', says one writer. The president who 'recklessly and flagrantly disregarded science and factual information' has had his viral comeuppance. We have some 'justification' for considering Trump's contraction of coronavirus 'to be a kind of karmic retribution', says a writer for the *Guardian*. It is retribution, he suggests, for Trump's 'irresponsible pursuit of partisan advantage over the national interest'.

'Karmic retribution' is, of course, only a slightly more PC, hippyish way to say what people in medieval times thought about plagues: that they were divine punishment. Punishment of avaricious individuals or of entire sinful communities. A key metaphor in this pre-modern understanding of plagues-as-retribution was that these judgemental diseases were inescapable. No one – not Pharaohs, not the wealthy, not even a reality-TV star who becomes the most powerful man in the world – could hide from their pox-ridden reprimands. As Susan Sontag wrote in her masterful *AIDS and its Metaphors* (1989), the pre-modern view of disease as retribution was an 'essential vehicle for the most pessimistic reading' of humanity's capacity. '[T]he standard plague story was of inexorability, *inescapability*', she wrote. This insistence on inescapability, on the plague as discoverer of all sinners, wherever they cower and lurk, infuses the cynically joyous commentary on Trump's illness. 'Fate leads the willing, Seneca said, while the unwilling get dragged', writes Dowd. *Fate.* That pre-Renaissance idea. It's back.

This is all 'karmic irony', says a writer for CNN. In this 'plague year', he says, 'the president who downplayed the pandemic for so long and dismissed the wearing of masks has come down with the disease'. The inhabitants of the Twittersphere have been even more unrestrained in their pre-modern relish at Trump's smiting by coronavirus, including a former staffer for Hillary Clinton, who said she hopes he dies. Well, he deserves to, right, for his blasphemous questioning of the seriousness of Covid and the efficacy of masking and locking down? In the words of Dowd, the most retributive of the new priestly class, 'the president's pernicious deceptions [have] boomeranged on him'. Nancy Pelosi says Trump's bristling against expert advice on Covid was a 'brazen invitation' to the sickness to visit his own home. Question and ye shall be visited ...

And so shall a plague cover the land of Trump. That is what these people are saying. They have imbued Covid with moral power and even political authority. For the sins that Trump is apparently being judged for, apparently being sickened for, are fundamentally political ones. It is not merely that he has refused to wear a mask or has questioned the wisdom of lockdowns. Enforced masking and the shutdown of economic life that we have seen across much of the Western world are strategies about which it is entirely legitimate (or ought to be) to have differing points of view, to have reasoned, rational debates about efficacy and impact. No, Trump's chief sin is a larger one than that: it is that he has bristled against the rule of experts and the contemporary liberal orthodoxy that says science has all the answers to our political and moral problems. This is the true thoughtcrime for which Covid has apparently infected Trump.

'Reality bursts the Trumpworld bubble', as the *New York Times'* headline puts it. 'The one-time reality-TV star has run smack into scientific reality', says CNN. This might sound modern and sciency, but it is little different to when priests of old insisted that visitations of the pox were a case of people's sinful behaviour crashing into God's judgement. And it isn't only Trump who has sinned, of course; so have his allegedly clueless, scientifically illiterate supporters. Much of the 'karmic retribution' commentary sees them as being reprimanded by the plague as much as Trump. It is Trumpworld that might finally be roused to normalcy by Trump's sickness, in the words of the *Times*. Hopefully Trump's smiting will be a 'wake-up call' to his supporters, says CNN with typical sniffyness. 'Perhaps Trump's illness will ... be seen to have provided a much-needed national wake-up call', says Geoffrey Kabaservice in the *Guardian*. Lord knows, the masses of 'Trumpworld' need a wake-up call, those maskless, expert-questioning brain sinners. They are to the technocratic, 'evidence'-led rule of the new clerisy what the deviants of Gomorrah were to God's writ.

CNN cut to the chase in one of its commentaries on Trump's Covid diagnosis. The true sickness in America, it said, is the 'sickness of hyper-partisanship'. And of course Trump is most responsible for this diseased form of politics, which 'too often elevates cruelty and justifies lies, through a vision of politics as a version of civil war'. Covid might be a serious virus, but what America really needs is 'healing from hyper-partisanship ... if we're going to see something resembling real healing in the American body politic'.

This is what's really going on here: Covid's judgement, this plague-like retribution, is being marshalled by the old technocratic elites as a cudgel against what are presumed to be Trumpworld's chief moral errors. The scepticism about lockdown, the broader doubting that experts have all the answers to our moral and political dilemmas,

the temerity to clarify the huge political differences between
ordinary people and the woke elites (what CNN refers to as
'the sickness of hyper-partisanship') – this is what the plague
is apparently admonishing. Isn't that funny? That a random virus
should give retributive voice to the pre-existing views and prejudices
of the liberal elites? The progressive view embodied by Sontag –
that disease is 'not a curse, not a punishment, not an embarrassment
– *without meaning*' – has been replaced by the view of Covid as
lethal reproachment for the sins of Trumpism, the ills of politics,
and the thoughtcrimes of dissenters in 21st-century America.

Strikingly, this isn't the first time that Biblical metaphors have
been deployed to chastise Trump and his supporters. Just a couple
of weeks ago, the fires on the west coast of the US were heralded
as heated punishment for Trumpworld's thoughtcrimes against
science. These flames were the direct consequence of Trump and
his supporters' temerity in questioning climate-change alarmism,
we were told. In mid-September the *New York Times* – which then
viewed fire rather than plague as the master reprimander of the
inhabitants of Trumpworld – discussed the fires in the context of
Trump once again rejecting science. Joe Biden went further, calling
Trump a 'climate arsonist'. Trump's doubt about the manmade
climate-change narrative will set America 'ablaze', said Biden.
Suburban neighbourhoods will be 'flooded out', suburbs will be
'blown away in superstorms', and homes will be 'burned in wildfires'.

And there you have it, in Biblical writ: if Trump stays in power,
America will be visited by floods, fires and plagues; death will
come to your door; pestilence will be visited upon the land. This
pre-modernism among those who fancy themselves as modern –
as enlightened and 'woke' – is striking. It speaks to their own
profound inability to come up with a vision for the US that might
inspire voters, so instead they must invoke a PC version of Leviticus
and warn people that if you don't choose us then you will be
consumed by hellfire and disease. And it confirms what they find
so distasteful about so-called Trumpworld – the fact that it has
dared to question expert authority, pushed aside the liberal elites
who believe that they are the only people sensible enough to rule,

and propagated the apparently outrageous idea that ordinary people (eurgh) have something to contribute to the discussion about how we deal with Covid-19 and other crises.

This is what lurks behind the irrational, anti-Enlightened treatment of Covid as a metaphor for the sicknesses of 21st-century America – the desperation of the bruised old elites to regain their authority over a people whom they view as too dumb, vulgar and destructive to govern their own lives. Now that's sick.

5 OCTOBER 2020

KAMALA HARRIS: ESTABLISHMENT IDENTITARIAN

TOM SLATER

'I'm speaking.' So said Democratic vice-presidential nominee
Kamala Harris, repeatedly, during the 2020 VP debate. She was
trying and failing to present Republican Mike Pence as an incessant
mansplainer, even while he was being unflinchingly, occasionally
creepily, courteous. ('Thank you, Susan' was his stock response
to almost every question from moderator Susan Page.)

Kamala Harris could well be the 47th president of the United
States. Her running mate, Joe Biden, whose recent gaffes include
confusing his wife for his sister, is thought unlikely to seek a second
term, if indeed he wins in November, given his advanced years and
growing fogginess. There is even speculation as to whether he will
make it through the first four years.

Given that Donald Trump, three years Biden's junior at 74, is
already the oldest first-term US president in history, and was recently
hospitalised with coronavirus, the vice-presidential debate took
on more significance this year. In Pence and Harris the American
people are looking at potential commanders-in-chief, rather than
just the understudies.

Other than the fly that landed on Pence's head, and stayed
there for a mesmerising two minutes, Harris's sassy deflections
of the vice-president's non-interruptions were key moments of
the night. And not in a good way. While liberal cable-news channels
clipped the exchanges, and Twitter proclaimed 'SLAY KWEEN',
I'm sure many voters were reminded of the kind of identitarian
posturing from Democrats that they have come to loathe.

Harris has particular form in this regard, proving herself willing to throw around accusations of bigotry (and worse) to score political points and damage her opponents. Even her running mate hasn't been spared this. In one debate during the Democratic primary, she essentially called Joe Biden a racist over his former opposition to bussing. She also said, prior to the primaries, that she 'believed' the women who had accused him of inappropriate conduct.

Where Harris is concerned, identity is essentially her entire pitch. Ever since she was selected as Biden's VP, making her the first woman of colour on a major presidential ticket, she has been talked up incessantly as an 'inspiration'. Even though the main people she seems to give a warm feeling to are Democratic grandees and liberal commentators: she flamed out of the primary after failing to pick up support among women and black voters.

Still, she continues to play the part. She often talks about her background, as the daughter of Jamaican and Indian immigrants, and is given to talking in the mode of an inspirational Instagrammer. In a recent profile in *Elle*, she tells a story about her falling out of her stroller at a march as a child, and her mother then trying to comfort her: 'She's like, "Baby, what do you want? What do you need?" And I just looked at her and I said, "Fweedom".'

This and other improbable, cringeworthy anecdotes are used to underline that Harris has been fighting her entire life. But what she is fighting for is still not entirely clear. She talks almost entirely in wispy platitudes. In a long interview with the *New York Times* last year, she talked more about potholes than policy. As the *Times* revealingly concluded, she is a 'messenger whose message remains a work in progress'.

Meanwhile, she has been dogged by her record as district attorney of San Francisco and attorney general of California, which gives the lie to her claims to be a 'progressive prosecutor'. Despite her vocal support for Black Lives Matter, critics say she resisted investigating police shootings. She also launched a brutal crackdown on truancy that dragged poor parents through the courts, even when their child was only out of school due to chronic health problems.

It would be unkind to suggest Harris is a principle-free politician who changes her mind purely on the basis of political expediency.

But that is almost certainly the case. In 2009, she said she wanted more cops on the street. In the wake of the killing of George Floyd, she derided that position as 'status-quo thinking' and 'just wrong'. During a primary debate, she raised her hand in support of abolishing private health insurance, only to claim later that she misheard the question.

Identity politics is often caricatured as the preserve of the far left. But some of its keenest practitioners are often those on the centrist, technocratic left. The therapeutic, woke blather of people like Harris provides a progressive-sounding gloss to what is often the same old establishment politics, primarily interested in maintaining power. It makes a candidate beloved by the Democratic elite, Wall Street and Big Tech appear momentarily, superficially progressive.

Harris may be the future of the Democratic Party. But this is a future that looks a hell of a lot like the past — technocratic, aloof, only a lot more cringey.

9 OCTOBER 2020

THE RISE OF 'ACCEPTABLE' CONSPIRACY THEORIES

TIM BLACK

Many at the liberal, right-thinking centre of public discourse openly oppose conspiracy theories. As you might expect they would.

They hold up the QAnon tale of Satan-worshipping paedophiles running a deep-state operation against President Trump and rightly ridicule it. They take the proliferating stories of 5G evil, including the bizarre claim that Covid-19 has been emitted by phone masts, and eviscerate them. And they round on the idea that today's pandemic is in fact a 'plandemic', orchestrated by Bill Gates, the World Health Organisation and Big Pharma, and take it apart.

And rightly so. Criticism of the conspiratorial mindset and its products is vital. Doing so challenges the reduction of complex, real-world events and problems to the handiwork of an evil cabal or group. It shows how conspiracy theory yields no understanding, let alone solutions. Instead, as our experience of the 20th century shows, it produces scapegoats. And often tragically so.

Yet, while the ideas surrounding QAnon or the 'plandemic' are routinely blasted by many in the comfortable, liberal slipstream of society, these self-same opponents of conspiracy theories often seem oblivious to the conspiratorial beam in their own eye.

For a start, they tend to view conspiracy theories in an increasingly conspiratorial way – as the products of 'right-wing' or 'far-right' groups funded by 'dark money'. Conspiracy theories, they say, fester in the darker corners of social media and the internet, seizing hold of the imaginations of the powerless, frustrated and embittered. By which such critics mean Trump supporters and Brexit voters.

Such a portrait of the conspiratorial mindset, painted as an affliction of the right-wing and supposedly low-information, allows commentators to ignore what has become blindingly obvious over the past few years – namely, that conspiracy theories are just as prevalent on the dinner-party circuit as they are in the darker corners of the internet.

Perhaps the most glaring example of the 'acceptable' conspiracy theory is that which reduces Brexit and Trump to the machinations of a perfidious cabal of devilish geeks and far-right whizzes, helped out with a dollop of Russian state aid. At the centre of this conspiracy theory is usually a tech company established by the SCL group, called Cambridge Analytica, which supposedly harvested the personal Facebook data of millions of users, bewitched them with targeted ads, and subsequently swung the EU referendum vote and the 2016 US election in favour of Brexit and Trump respectively.

So acceptable in mainstream circles is this rather incredible tale that peddling it won prizes for the *Observer* and Carole Cadwalladr, and publishing contracts for assorted mediocrities determined to restore the pre-2016 status quo.

But when Elizabeth Denham, Britain's information commissioner, finally published the conclusions of her three-year-long investigation into what the *Observer* had once called 'The Great British Brexit Robbery', she found there had been no robbery.

Denham declared that she had found 'no further evidence to change my earlier view that SCL / CA were not involved in the EU referendum campaign in the UK'. And as to Putin's dastardly role, Denham was just as unequivocal, saying there was no 'additional evidence of Russian involvement'. As Josh Glancy put it in *The Sunday Times*: 'In conclusion, the devilish techniques flogged by Cambridge Analytica were oversold and commonly available, had no impact on Brexit and were not connected to Russia in any meaningful way.'

In other words, Britain's information commissioner has officially exposed the story of the hackers who won Brexit at Putin's behest for what it always was: a conspiracy theory. It was a tale just as post-truth, as demented and as damaging to public discourse, as anything purveyed by the bedroom-dwelling fringes of the internet. But unlike the advocates of, say, the plandemic, those who indulge fantasies of Putin as the dark-moneyed power behind the thrones of Trump and Johnson are not censored on social media, or ridiculed in polite society. They are praised, feted and all-platformed.

Likewise, while those claiming that Hillary Clinton is heading a paedophile ring are rightly ridiculed and shunned, LBC's James O'Brien, the pathologically smug broadcaster who long championed the daft tale of a Westminster paedophile ring, continues to be hailed, albeit largely by himself, as a voice of reason.

It seems that some conspiracy theories are more acceptable than others. And herein lies the problem. A conspiracy theory is only criticised when its advocates are already deemed beyond the pale. But when its advocates are centrist mainstays, when the conspiracy theory in question, no matter how warped and malicious, plays to the centrist crowd, then the conspiratorial mindset is ignored. Indeed, in the case of Cadwalladr and the *Observer*, the conspiracy theory is embraced, celebrated and advanced – even after the information commissioner has debunked it.

We can see this happening again in relation to coronavirus. Scientists and public figures who have come out in opposition to further lockdown restrictions being imposed on social life are now said to be in the pay of shadowy vested interests. Their perfectly legitimate positions are attributed to the evil capitalists said to be intent on letting Covid-19 wipe out the aged and infirm. Take the response to the Great Barrington Declaration, which expressed the 'grave concerns' of 'epidemiologists and public-health scientists' about 'the damaging physical and mental-health impacts of the prevailing Covid-19 policies'. The *Guardian* stated that these scientists, from Oxford, Harvard and Stanford, had been 'co-opted by shady ideological interests'. *Byline Times* said the declaration was the product of 'an opaque lobbying effort', and dismissed it as 'predatory neoliberal economics in disguise'.

It is difficult to overestimate the damage being done to public discussion and debate by conspiracy theorising – especially its acceptable, broadsheet variety, which hasn't been criticised nearly enough. We have seen how it leads to the demonisation of public figures, conjured up as child abusers. We have seen how, for too long, it justified the undermining of the democratic vote for Brexit.

And now we see how it is shutting down debate about the response to the pandemic, the most important issue of our time.

It's not enough simply to criticise the bonkers conspiracy theories of the fringe right. We also have to challenge the presence of the conspiratorial mindset at the heart of the political and cultural establishment.

13 OCTOBER 2020

JE SUIS SAMUEL

BRENDAN O'NEILL

Yesterday, cancel culture turned murderous. It became positively medieval. On a suburban street on the outskirts of Paris a schoolteacher was beheaded in broad daylight for the supposed crime of showing caricatures of Muhammad to his pupils during a classroom discussion about freedom of speech. Decapitated for dissing the prophet, in France, in the 21st century. In essence, the teacher was cancelled, in the most thorough and depraved way imaginable. Enough is enough — everyone must now stand against all snivelling apologists for censorship and cancellation and defend unfettered freedom of speech as the cornerstone of civilised society.

The news from France was truly grim. Samuel Paty, a 47-year-old teacher of history and geography at a middle school in Conflans-Sainte-Honorine, was murdered and beheaded by an 18-year-old Chechen Islamic extremist. The murderous censor was heard yelling out 'Allahu Akbar'. Then we discovered why Mr Paty was slaughtered in such a deranged, pre-modern fashion: because he dared to show some of *Charlie Hebdo*'s cartoons of Muhammad to his pupils during a lesson on why the liberties of thought and speech are so essential to the French Republic. That he reportedly offered his Muslim pupils the opportunity to leave the classroom while the Muhammad caricatures were being discussed wasn't enough to protect him from the 7th-century fury of his executioner, who no doubt felt 'offended' by Mr Paty's behaviour.

Every Islamic extremist attack over the past five years has been shocking and disturbing. In France alone, around 250 people have been massacred by radical Islamists since 2015. But there is something especially horrific about the premeditated targeting of a teacher for doing his job — that is, encouraging his pupils to think critically. Parents of his pupils say he was a kind, enthusiastic teacher who always encouraged children to think about issues in depth. Sophie Vénétitay of the SNES-FSU teachers' union was right to say that he was murdered for doing what good teachers are meant to do – 'teach critical thought'. This attack targeted one man, but its aim was to terrorise an entire republic; to send a dire, Middle Ages-style warning to public servants that they will put themselves in danger if they dare, in the terrorist's own words, to 'belittle Muhammad'.

So Mr Paty was beheaded for the crime of blasphemy. He was the victim of a barbaric one-man inquisition. Yet even as we balk at the depravity of this act of terror, we also have to confront the fact that it did not take place in a vacuum. Nor did the massacre at *Charlie Hebdo*'s offices five years ago, or the barely discussed attack with a meat cleaver carried out by a Pakistani man at the site of *Charlie Hebdo*'s old offices just three weeks ago, in which two people were wounded. No, all of these attacks, all of these explicit acts of vengeance for the supposed speechcrime of 'blaspheming' against Muhammad, took place in an era in which criticism of Islam is described as 'Islamophobia' and in which offending Muslims is apparently one of the worst things you can do. There's a context to these barbaric attacks – it's the context of the cult of cancellation and the ridiculous, regressive idea that people have a right not to be offended.

These attacks are an expression of two of the most worrying trends in Western European societies right now: Islamic extremism and cancel culture. Strikingly, open, frank discussion of both of these problems is constantly discouraged by the political and cultural elites. After Islamic-extremist attacks we are implored not to look back in anger, to forget about it, essentially, and move on. Dwell for too long on something like the Manchester Arena bombing in 2017 or the Nice truck attack on Bastille Day in 2016 and you run the risk of being branded 'Islamophobic', that catch-all term of demonisation that is designed to chill debate about radical Islam, the crisis of integration, and the social and cultural divisions fostered by the ideology of multiculturalism. As for cancel culture, it doesn't exist, the chattering classes tell us; it's the concoction of right-wing culture warriors who just don't like being 'called out'.

But these things do exist. Islamic extremism is a genuine problem in 21st-century Europe and the trend for cancelling people deemed guilty of wrongthink — whether it's feminists who question aspects of transgenderism or people concerned about mass immigration — is a real and growing phenomenon. Indeed, cancel culture is applied with particular vigour against anyone who criticises Islam. They will be branded 'phobic' or racist. People have lost their jobs and even been dragged to court in European countries for 'blaspheming' against Muhammad. And who can forget the reluctance of significant sections of the cultural establishment — including columnists and novelists — to stand by *Charlie Hebdo* following the massacre of many of its cartoonists and writers in 2015? Sure, no one should have been killed, they said, but that magazine *is* 'Islamophobic'; it 'punches down', whatever the hell that means.

All these spineless excuse-makers for religious censorship, all these people who failed time and again to stand with people who were being chastised, censured or even physically attacked for questioning or making fun of Islam, ought to be taking a long, hard look in the mirror this morning. For they have contributed to this climate in which extremists take it upon themselves to punish 'blasphemers'. The elites' mainstreaming of the idea of 'Islamophobia', their treatment of criticism of Islam as a racist scourge that must be cancelled, gives a green light to Islamists to take even more punishing action against anyone who dares to disrespect their religion. The terrible truth is this: the No Platforming of people for being critical of Islam and the murder of people for being critical of Islam differ only by degree, only by severity. In both cases, the exact same warped ideology is being applied: that it is legitimate to punish 'offensive' speech, especially if it is offensive to some Muslims.

The beheading of Mr Paty was a militarised expression of cancel culture. That killer was the armed wing of political correctness, a self-styled enforcer of the now mainstream idea that it is 'phobic' (that is, evil) to criticise Islam. Indeed, the interplay between the mainstream chilling of discussion about Islam and the extremist attacks on individuals who 'blaspheme' against Islam can be seen in the fact that Mr Paty was the subject of complaints from parents before he became the target of a murderous terrorist.

Indeed, it seems he only came to the attention of his executioner because of a social-media fuss over his lessons on freedom of speech. The everyday instinct for cancelling problematic people feeds the monster of extremist violent censorship.

'Freedom of speech has consequences' — that is the *cri de coeur* of the censorious woke left and the illiberal cultural elites. Well, guess what? It will have been the *cri de coeur* of the piece of shit who murdered Mr Paty, too. That oh-so-common cry that free speech has consequences is one of the most chilling ideas of our time. It doesn't mean that freedom of speech has the consequence of disagreement and debate and ridicule, of people using *their* speech to challenge *your* speech — this is something all of us accept and actively welcome. No, it means that if you express certain ideas, you will suffer. Make no mistake: *it is a threat.* Speak your mind and you will suffer the consequences — job loss, banishment from campus, public shaming, even hounding in the streets, as we have seen in recent furious confrontations between correct-thinking mobs and people who dare to hold different opinions. All that radical Islamists do is add a further 'consequence' to freedom of speech — extrajudicial execution.

Enough is enough. If the slaying of Samuel Paty doesn't act as a wake-up call to the censorious elites, then we really are in serious trouble. Teaching unions across Europe should absolutely condemn his murder and defend the right of teachers and professors to challenge their pupils and students, including with caricatures of Muhammad. Campuses must cease all their regressive No Platforming and speech-policing policies. Cancel culture needs to be cancelled. And we need to *normalise* criticism of Islam — alongside criticism of Christianity and every other religion — in order to send a clear message to everyone: that no god, prophet, faith or fad is beyond questioning in our free societies. Let's all say 'Je suis Samuel' and confront the apologists who created this world in which people fantasise that they have a right not to be offended.

17 OCTOBER 2020

JACINDAMANIA

JOANNA WILLIAMS

Could Jacinda Ardern be more loved? New Zealand's prime minister led her party to a landslide victory in the recent General Election, winning 64 out of 120 seats and scoring the Labour Party's best performance in five decades. But it's not just New Zealanders who are celebrating – the whole world seems gripped by Jacindamania.

World leaders have queued up to declare their love. Boris Johnson tweeted his congratulations, adding 'the UK and NZ have great things to look forward to'. London mayor Sadiq Khan said he and Ardern shared a vision 'for an inclusive, fairer and greener future'. Justin Trudeau went one better, tweeting, 'There's so much we can do together and I'm looking forward to all of it' (which I find kind of creepy, but each to their own). Even the Dalai Lama got in on the act: 'I admire the courage, wisdom and leadership [of Jacinda Ardern], as well as the calm, compassion and respect for others she has shown in these challenging times.'

What's strange is that the result of an election in a country with 5.6 sheep to every human (down from a peak of 22 sheep per person in 1982), and a population smaller than Yorkshire, should attract such global attention.

Explanations are not in short supply. Jacinda Ardern is a woman. She's young(ish). And she's cool. The contrast between Ardern and the geriatric men who've been slogging it out to become US president most definitely helps keep the love coming.

But dig deeper and it's clear that what really drives Jacindamania is that Ardern is not a populist. She has long been heralded as a challenge to so-called strongmen like Trump and Bolsonaro. Her victory – and the resounding defeat of newly formed populist party Advance NZ – is taken as a sign that the public has rejected 'populism, conspiracy theories and scepticism about Covid-19'. Advance NZ won just 0.9 per cent of the vote. Interestingly, even Labour devotees attribute its victory over Advance, in part, to the absence of the 'Murdoch press' in New Zealand and the fact that, two days before the election, Facebook removed Advance NZ's page from its platform for spreading Covid-19 misinformation. Even Ardern's fans seem to think it was these factors that won it for her, rather than any particular vision she may have for her party and the country.

It is easy to see why the tub-thumpers in Britain's own Labour Party, having recently overseen their own party's biggest electoral defeat in almost a century, are seeking solace in the knowledge that someone, somewhere, however insignificant, can lead a vaguely left-of-centre party to victory. But it is still worth asking: what exactly does Ardern's Labour Party stand for? After one full term as prime minister there still seems to be little sense of her party's vision. Instead, the vacuum at the heart of the New Zealand government is successfully covered up with the authoritarian, the woke and the twee.

Ardern's electoral success is mostly put down to her handling of the coronavirus pandemic. Only 25 New Zealanders have died from Covid-19 and the country has slowly emerged from lockdown. As part of Ardern's widely praised 'elimination strategy', New Zealand was placed under a strict national lockdown on 25 March. At this point, there had been only 102 recorded cases of Covid-19 in the country and not one single death. Ardern insisted she was 'not willing to put the lives of her citizens in danger' and closed the national border. Since the middle of March, only a tiny number of people have been able to enter New Zealand, and even then under strict quarantine rules.

The cost of this widely celebrated authoritarianism is that New Zealand's biggest export industry − tourism − has imploded. Prior to coronavirus, tourism directly generated 5.8 per cent of GDP and indirectly contributed to an additional four per cent. Over eight per cent of New Zealanders worked in tourism. Not any more. Many of these people are now out of work and the collapse of tourism is one of the main reasons why New Zealand's economy is now heading into recession for the first time in several decades. But for those on the lockdown left – those who see no contradiction in supporting free movement in Europe one minute and celebrating New Zealand pulling up the national drawbridge the next – throwing so many people out of work is a small price to pay for demonstrating the success of their favoured approach to tackling coronavirus.

No matter how deep New Zealand's forthcoming recession, and how high the levels of unemployment, all will no doubt be forgiven – abroad if not at home – because Ardern shares the same woke values as every other member of the global elite.

Prior to the pandemic, Ardern received international praise for her response to the horrific right-wing terror attack on two mosques in Christchurch, in which 51 people were brutally murdered. Ardern not only condemned the attack but also refused to say the attacker's name in parliament, declaring instead her wish that the names of the victims should live on. Images of Ardern, hair covered with a scarf, hugging relatives and kissing survivors, were beamed around the world.

According to the *Guardian*, Ardern's obvious compassion was all the more significant 'at a time when governments in Europe and the United States are either brazenly anti-Muslim and xenophobic or at best silent on the matter of immigration and Islam'. What's notable is that so many British commentators clearly felt far more comfortable praising Ardern's response to the Christchurch attack than they did commemorating the victims of the Manchester Arena bombing, or those of any of the other Islamist terror attacks that have taken place in the UK.

Ardern's authoritarianism is sugar-coated in love, while the devastating economic recession comes with a side order of woke. This, it seems, is enough to keep Jacindamania buzzing. She might enter a coalition with the Greens! There are now more gay members of parliament in New Zealand than in any other parliament on Earth!

But if Ardern plays to the admiration of the global opinion-forming set, rather than listening to the citizens of New Zealand, things might look very different when the next General Election comes along.

19 OCTOBER 2020

THE TYRANNY OF BIG TECH

FRASER MYERS

The *New York Post*'s Hunter Biden exposé is arguably the most important story of the election – not the allegations themselves, but the attempt to suppress them. The story adds more detail and evidence to allegations that are by now well known about Hunter Biden's wheeler-dealing in Ukraine, allegedly trading off his father's name, perhaps with his father's knowledge. But the attempts to suppress the story have revealed the totalitarian impulses of those who hold a near monopoly on the flow of information – and on whose behalf they are willing to exercise their power.

There are many reasonable ways the Joe Biden campaign could have responded to the exposé. It could have ignored it or dismissed it as a last-ditch attempt at mudslinging from the Trump camp. It could have countered it by pointing out Trump's brazen nepotism, such as him bringing his daughter Ivanka and son-in-law Jared Kushner into the White House. It could have drowned it out by pointing to the extensive allegations of corruption against the president and his administration. But Biden and the Democrats didn't need to do any of that, because the elites of Silicon Valley are on their side and were willing to try to crush the story entirely.

In the weeks since the *Post* broke its story, it has been locked out of its Twitter account, meaning that America's oldest daily newspaper is forbidden from sharing any of its articles. When the story came out, Twitter users (including editors from the *Post*) were prevented from tweeting links to the report, posting photos of it and even sending it in private messages. Some tweets to the report managed to slip through before Twitter's censors sprang into action. These were then slapped with a warning message. At first, users were told the article was 'potentially harmful'. This was then updated to say it was 'potentially spammy or unsafe'. Twitter had decided on behalf of the voters that there was nothing to see here.

Facebook also suppressed the story. Communications director Andy Stone announced that 'we are reducing its distribution on our platform' as part of 'our standard process to reduce the spread of misinformation'. The story was 'eligible to be fact-checked', but no one, it seems, was willing to do so. As many have pointed out, numerous sensationalist, unverified stories about Trump have appeared in the mainstream media (from the Steele dossier to the many Russiagate non-bombshells) that later turned out to be untrue. Yet none of these was deemed 'eligible' for Facebook's 'fact-checking'.

Part of this eagerness to censor comes from the fact that so many in the liberal establishment blame social media for the Trump upset in 2016. Not the Democrats' disastrous choice of candidate or her sneering, tick-box campaign. Not the public's broader rejection of the technocratic, establishment politics Hillary Clinton embodied, which, far from bringing rationality and harmony, brought financial crises, endless bloody wars and soaring inequality. But Facebook.

Ironically, of course, when Obama was re-elected in 2012, Facebook was seen as a force for good. The liberal establishment was excited by the first true 'social-media election'. Social media and big data were said to have made 'elections smarter' and 'restored the soul of politics'. But the election of Trump represented such a system shock that a scapegoat had to be found. Something had to be done about the voters expressing their wrong opinions and reading things that might give them the wrong ideas.

Over the past four years, this has led to tremendous external pressure on the tech companies – and an internal willingness – to censor, block and regulate what is said on their platforms. Politicians, campaigners, journalists and assorted do-gooders demanded greater checks on 'misinformation' and 'hateful' language. The ousting of undesirables like Alex Jones, Milo Yiannopoulos and Katie Hopkins (alongside some feminists for good measure) was cheered on by the illiberal liberals. But it didn't end with them, of course. Back in 2012, Twitter's general manager hailed the platform as belonging to 'the free-speech wing of the free-speech party'. By 2020, Twitter was censoring the tweets of the elected president of the United States. Some of Trump's claims about looting and Covid-19 have been hidden behind warning signs.

Given that terms like 'misinformation' and 'hate' are inherently subjective, it is hardly surprising that the targets of censorship are not evenly distributed across the political spectrum. Silicon Valley is dominated by woke liberals, hence it is those who challenge woke, liberal views who are most likely to be censored (though left-wingers are by no means safe).

What if the roles had been reversed? Can you imagine if, instead of embracing Biden, Silicon Valley's finest had supported Trump instead? Can you envisage the reaction if Google or Twitter banned content critical of Trump and the Republican Party, while actively promoting content critical of Biden and the Democrats? This would be widely, and rightly, understood as an affront to democracy. But when the liberal establishment is determined to correct the 'mistake' of 2016 at all costs, all principles are thrown out of the window.

And it's not just tech that is acting as a gatekeeper, looking to squash any story that might hurt Biden or aid Trump in the run-up to the election. Beyond the right-wing, partisan media, most outlets have refused to cover or investigate the Hunter story in any great detail. NPR could not even acknowledge that it was a story, declaring it a 'pure distraction' that would waste its journalists' and listeners' time. CNN's Christiane Amanpour said that reporting or investigating the story would be 'doing [the Trump campaign's] work'.

Other outlets have dismissed the story as 'Russian disinformation'. Alleging connections to Russia has now become a well-established method of discrediting any story, candidate or election outcome that is distasteful to the establishment. A *Washington Post* editorial was at least honest when it brazenly declared: 'We must treat the Hunter Biden leaks as if they were a foreign intelligence operation – even if they probably aren't.'

The implications for after the election are stark. The same press outlets that have studiously avoided critical coverage of Biden on the campaign trail would assume responsibility for challenging and scrutinising a potential Biden presidency. Who is to say they wouldn't bury an inconvenient truth again if they feared it would benefit the other side? And who is to say their friends in Big Tech wouldn't help them out if they decided to do so?

The elites of the old and new media have not just turned against Trump. They have also turned against democracy itself.

29 OCTOBER 2020

THE REAL RESISTANCE

BRENDAN O'NEILL

So Joe Biden has won the highest popular vote in the history of the US. At the time of writing, more than 73million people have voted for him. He has beaten the record set by Barack Obama who was swept to power with 69.5million votes in 2008. But here's the thing: so has Donald Trump. At the time of writing, he has 69.7million votes. So he has won the second-highest popular vote in the history of the American republic. That is remarkable.

Why? For one simple reason. Trump is the man we're all meant to hate. He has been raged against ceaselessly by the cultural elites for the past four years. Hardly any of the American media backed him in 2020. Globalist institutions loathe him. Academia, the media elites, the social-media oligarchies, the celebrity set and other hugely influential sectors have branded him a 21st-century Hitler.

And still, around 70million Americans voted for him.

That is what makes the vote for Trump so important. Because what it speaks to is the existence of vast numbers of people who are outside of the purview of the cultural elites. People who have developed some kind of immunity to the cultural supremacy of the 'woke' worldview so intensely mainstreamed by the political and media sets in recent years. People who are more than content to defy the diktats of the supposedly right-thinking elites and cast their ballots in a way that they think best tallies with their political, social and class interests. People who, to varying degrees, are at least sceptical towards the narratives of identitarianism, racial doom-mongering, climate-change hysteria and all the pronouns nonsense that are essentially the new ideology of the ruling class.

Hillary Clinton infamously referred to Trump supporters as 'the deplorables'. But a far better word for them would be 'the unconquerables'. These are minds and hearts uncolonised by the new orthodoxies. Seventy million people in a peaceful state of revolt against the new establishment and its eccentric, authoritarian ideologies. This is the most important story of the us election and it deserves serious attention.

The fury of the elites in the wake of the us election is palpable. Already there is rage against the innate racism and 'white supremacy' of the throng. Already there is neo-racist disgust with the Latinos and black people who, in larger numbers than in 2016, voted for Trump. 'We are surrounded by racists', said *New York Times* columnist Charles M Blow. This rage of the elites against the masses, despite the victory of the elites' preferred candidate, suggests they instinctively recognise their failure to bring significant sections of the masses to heel.

The elites have been thrown by this election. First, because they called it so wrongly. Their polls and punditry insisting that Trumpism would be resoundingly defeated turned out to be incorrect. The stories of a 10-point swing to Biden evaporated upon contact with reality. So far, Trump has increased his vote by around seven million.

The elite's wrongness about the election is itself a crushing confirmation of its failure ideologically to domesticate large numbers of Americans. Many ordinary people have clearly chosen not to communicate their beliefs to pollsters, a key part of the new political clerisy, because they are aware that the political elites hold them in contempt. They know it's a waste of time. That is the size of the chasm that now exists between the guardians of correct-thought and millions of people.

The second reason this election has rattled the seeming victors is because of *who* voted for Trump. Exit polls suggest there were significant shifts of black and Latino voters to Trump. It is reported that 18 per cent of black men voted for Trump, up from the five per cent who voted for John McCain in 2008 and the 11 per cent who voted for Mitt Romney in 2012. A shift of this kind towards a politician relentlessly described as a 'white supremacist' is very significant. According to the AP VoteCast, 35 per cent of Latinos seem to have voted for Trump. And a whopping 59 per cent of Native Hawaiians and 52 per cent of Native Americans and Alaska Natives opted for Trump. Seemingly these native peoples didn't

get the NYT, SNL, DNC message that Trump is a racist who hates
all non-white people.

There is already fierce denunciation of minority groups who
voted for Trump. They have sold out to 'white supremacy', woke
academics and columnists claim. Blow writes in the *New York Times*
that the Latino and black shift towards Trump is proof of the 'power
of the white patriarchy': 'Some people who have been historically
oppressed will stand with their oppressors.' That's a lot of words
to say 'Uncle Tom'. The anger with Latinos and blacks who voted
for Trump is motivated by a view of these people as traitors to their
race. In the rigid worldview of the identitarian elites, people are
not individuals or members of an economic class – they are mere
manifestations of race and ethnicity and they must act accordingly.
That many voters have clearly bristled at such racial fatalism is a
very positive development. Identity politics was dealt a blow in
this election, and the elites know it.

More striking still is the educational divide. A majority of people
whose educational level is high school or less voted for Trump,
while a majority of college graduates voted for Biden. Among white
voters, the divide is even more stark. Majorities of white men voted
for Trump, but among white men who didn't go to college 64 per cent
voted for Trump, while among white men who did go to college it was
only 52 per cent. Meanwhile, 60 per cent of white women who didn't
go to college voted for Trump, whereas 59 per cent of white women
who did go to college voted for Biden.

Naturally, some observers claim this is proof that clever people
voted for Biden while dumb people prefer Trump. In truth, this split
is primarily reflective of the key role universities now play as factories
of woke indoctrination. From critical race theory to genderfluidity,
from the view of American history as one crime after another to
the myopic policing of speech, universities have become important
transmitters of the ideologies of the new elites. As a consequence, one
of the great ironies of our time is that those who have not attended
a university seem better able to think independently and to resist
the coercions of elite-decreed correct-thought.

The ideas that hold on a university campus – that men can become
women, that controversial people must be 'cancelled', that describing
America as a 'melting pot' is offensive to non-white people – hold no

sway whatsoever in the factories, delivery centres, mess rooms or bars of vast swathes of America. That university-educated and non-university-educated people now think so differently is testament not to uneducated people's stupidity, but to the transformation of universities into machines for socialising young adults into the ways and creeds of the new elites.

Indeed, the split of Biden and Trump voters on issues is striking, too. Of the voters who think the economy and jobs is the most important issue, the vast majority are Trump supporters: 81 per cent compared with just 16 per cent who are Biden supporters. Of the voters who think racism is the most important issue, 78 per cent were Biden supporters and just 19 per cent Trump supporters. And of the voters who think climate change is the most important issue, 86 per cent were Biden supporters and just 11 per cent were Trump supporters. On Covid, of the voters who think it is 'not under control at all', 83 per cent were Biden supporters and just 15 per cent were Trump supporters.

This is incredibly revealing. On issues that are central to the clerisy's worldview, Trump voters deviate consistently from the elite narrative. That isn't to say they don't think climate change or racism are problems we must address – I'm sure majorities of them do. But they clearly reject the fatalism and dominance of these issues in the body politic. They clearly balk at the ceaseless discussions of America's inescapable racism and the idea that if Americans do not radically alter their lifestyles then they will fry in the heat-death of climate catastrophe. They push back against the identitarianism and apocalypticism of the new elites.

One study, published in the *Journal of Social and Political Psychology* after the 2016 election, hit on an important point: the evidence suggests that Trump-voting for many people was a form of 'cultural deviance ... [from] the salience of restrictive communication norms'. In short, the Trump phenomenon is a vehicle for those who don't agree that America is broken or racist, or that climate change will kill us all, or that identitarian correctness is more important than the economy and jobs.

Perhaps the most important act of 'cultural deviance' carried out by the millions who chose Trump over Biden is their attempt to re-elevate class over identity. This is why the shift of working-class blacks and Latinos towards Trump is so important. It is also why Trump voters' overwhelming belief that the economy and jobs is the most important issue in the US right now is so relevant. What we have witnessed in the US is a reassertion of the importance of class over identity, of the shared social and economic interests of a significant section of society over the narrow cultural obsessions of the new elites.

This is another reason why the elites are so furious after this election. It's the key reason, in fact. They instinctively recognise that the economic concerns, and, more importantly, the economic consciousness, of substantial sections of society pose a threat to their ideological dominance.

Corporations, the education system, the Democratic establishment, the media elites and the social-media oligarchies are heavily invested in the cult of identity because it is a means through which they can renew their economic dominance over society and exercise moral authority over the masses. Identitarianism has provided spiritual renewal for the capitalist elites, new means of rebuking and censuring the workforce in corporations, and a sense of purpose for a political class utterly adrift from the working masses it once sought to connect with. And they are not about to let some uppity blacks and Latinos and uneducated whites disrupt this new ruling-class ideology with their vulgar concerns about the economy and jobs.

Trump has lost. But so has the anti-Trump establishment. In some ways, the establishment's loss is more significant. These elites see in the 70million people who disobediently voted for 'evil' a genuine mass threat to their right to rule and their self-serving ideologies. And they are right to. For these unconquerables, these teeming millions who have not been captured by the new orthodoxies, are proof that populism will survive Trump's fall and that the self-protecting narratives of the new elites are not accepted by huge numbers of people.

This is the real resistance. Not the upper-middle-class TikTok revolutionaries and Antifa fantasists whose every view – on trans issues, Black Lives Matter, the wickedness of Trump – corresponds precisely with the outlook of Google and Nike and the *New York Times*.

No, the resistance is these working people. These defiant Hispanics. Those black men who did what black men are not supposed to do. Those non-college whites who think college ideologies are crazy. These people are the ones who have the balls and the independence of mind to force a serious rethink and realignment of the political sphere in the 21st-century West. More power to them.

6 NOVEMBER 2020

ABOUT THE AUTHORS

BRENDAN O'NEILL is editor of *spiked* and host of the *spiked* podcast, *The Brendan O'Neill Show*

TOM SLATER is deputy editor of *spiked*

TIM BLACK is editor of *spiked*'s long-reads

RAKIB EHSAN is a *spiked* columnist and research fellow at the Henry Jackson Society

JULIE BURCHILL is a journalist and author of *Welcome To The Woke Trials: How #Identity Killed Progressive Politics*, which will be published by Constable in 2021

ROB LYONS is a *spiked* columnist and science and technology director at the Academy of Ideas

PATRICK WEST is a *spiked* columnist and author of *Get Over Yourself: Nietzsche For Our Times*

SEAN COLLINS is *spiked*'s US correspondent

ANDREW DOYLE is a *spiked* columnist and host of the *spiked* podcast, *Culture Wars — with Andrew Doyle*

MICK HUME is a *spiked* columnist and author of *Trigger Warning: Is The Fear Of Being Offensive Killing Free Speech?*

JOANNA WILLIAMS is a *spiked* columnist and founder of the think tank, Cieo

FRASER MYERS is staff writer at *spiked* and host of the *spiked* podcast

PHIL MULLAN is author of *Beyond Confrontation: Globalists, Nationalists And Their Discontents*

WENDY KAMINER is a *spiked* columnist, lawyer and author

INAYA FOLARIN IMAN is a *spiked* columnist and founder of the Equiano Project

NICK CATER is a *spiked* columnist and executive director of the Menzies Research Centre

SABINE BEPPLER-SPAHL is *spiked*'s Germany correspondent

LUKE GITTOS is a *spiked* columnist and author of *Human Rights — Illusory Freedom: Why We Should Repeal The Human Rights Act*

WILFRED REILLY is a *spiked* columnist and author of *Taboo: 10 Facts You Can't Talk About*

CHRISTOPHER SNOWDON is head of lifestyle economics at the Institute of Economic Affairs and co-host of the *spiked* podcast, *Last Orders*

PADDY HANNAM is a *spiked* intern

ELLA WHELAN is a *spiked* columnist and author of *What Women Want: Fun, Freedom And An End To Feminism*

FRANK FUREDI is a sociologist and author of *Democracy Under Siege: Don't Let Them Lock It Down!*

sp!ked

spiked is the magazine that wants to change the world as well as report on it. Edited by Brendan O'Neill, and launched in 2001, it is irreverent where others conform, questioning where others wallow in received wisdom, and radical where others cling to the status quo.

At a time when it is fashionable to cancel 'problematic' people, to sideline voters when they give the 'wrong' answer, and to treat human beings as a drain on the planet, we make the case for human endeavour, the expansion of democracy, and freedom of speech with no ifs or buts.

Our motto is 'question everything' – or as the *New York Times* put it, we are 'the often-biting British publication fond of puncturing all manner of ideological balloons'. Read us every day at spiked-online.com.